The Grammar School Boys

SNOWBOUND

Dick & Co. at Winter Sports

H. IRVING HANCOCK

1st WORLD
LIBRARY
Literary Society

The Grammar School Boys Snowbound

H. Irving Hancock

© 1st World Library, 2009
PO Box 2211
Fairfield, IA 52556
www.1stworldlibrary.com
First Edition

LCCN: 2009923393

Softcover ISBN: 978-1-4218-8842-2
Hardcover ISBN: 978-1-4218-8941-2
eBook ISBN: 978-1-4218-8743-2

Purchase *"The Grammar School Boys Snowbound"*
as a traditional bound book at:
www.1stWorldLibrary.com/purchase.asp?ISBN=978-1-4218-8842-2

1st World Library is a literary, educational organization dedicated to:

- Creating a free internet library of downloadable ebooks

- Hosting writing competitions and offering book publishing scholarships.

Interested in more 1st World Library books? contact:
literacy@1stworldlibrary.com
Check us out at: www.1stworldlibrary.com

1st World Library Literary Society

Giving Back to the World

"If you want to work on the core problem, it's early school literacy."

- James Barksdale, former CEO of Netscape

"No skill is more crucial to the future of a child, or to a democratic and prosperous society, than literacy."

- Los Angeles Times

"Literacy... means far more than learning how to read and write... The aim is to transmit... knowledge and promote social participation."

- UNESCO

"Literacy is not a luxury, it is a right and a responsibility. If our world is to meet the challenges of the twenty-first century we must harness the energy and creativity of all our citizens."

- President Bill Clinton

"Parents should be encouraged to read to their children, and teachers should be equipped with all available techniques for teaching literacy, so the varying needs and capacities of individual kids can be taken into account."

- Hugh Mackay

CONTENTS

CHAPTER I

REALLY A GREAT PLAN, BUT…

As Hen Dutcher came up to a group of boys on the ice, and slowed down his speed, he stuck the point of his right skate in the ice to bring himself to a full stop.

"Huh! You fellows think you're some smart on fancy skating, don't you?" he demanded rather scornfully.

"No," replied Dave Darrin shortly.

"You been showing off a lot, then."

"Hen," grimaced Dave, "I'm afraid you're going to miss your calling in life."

"Didn't know I had any," grunted Hen.

"Yes, you have; one of your own choosing, too."

"What is it?" asked Hen curiously.

"You're a walking anvil chorus."

"An anvil chorus?" repeated Hen Dutcher, the puzzled

expression deepening in his face.

"Yes; wherever you go the fellows are sure to hear the sounds of 'hammering' and 'knocking.'"

A score of boys grinned, a dozen laughed outright. But Hen wasn't bright enough to see the point.

"What's an anvil got to do with it all?" demanded Hen in a puzzled tone. "An anvil belongs in a blacksmith shop."

"And that's where you ought to go, to do all your 'hammering' and 'knocking,'" explained Dave, as he skated slowly away.

"Huh! You think you're smart!" growled Hen, who still couldn't see why the other fellows had laughed.

"Hen," remarked Dick Prescott, "I'm afraid you're not up to concert pitch."

"Concert pitch?" repeated the dense one. "No, I know I'm not. Did I ever make any claim to being musical?"

"You see," hinted Greg Holmes, "the trouble with the Dutcher kid is that he's all ivory, from his collar-button up."

Another laugh greeted this assertion, but Hen only glared stupidly.

"Ivory is all white, anyway," Hen muttered. "So am I."

He swelled out his chest, did one or two fancy little things on skates, and tried to look important. But none of the other fellows in the group on the ice seemed inclined to take young Dutcher at his own valuation.

H. Irving Hancock

Hen Dutcher was a peculiar chap, at any rate. His worst fault, probably—but one that led to other faults—was his egotism. He was always thinking about himself and his own puny little interests. For the life of him, Hen couldn't understand why he wasn't popular with other fellows. He sometimes realized that he wasn't, but charged the fact up to the other fellows being "too stuck on themselves, or on those 'boobs,' Dick Prescott and Dave Darrin."

"Let's run Hen ashore and rub his face in the snow!" proposed one boy gleefully.

"You dassent!" flared up Hen. But half a dozen boys uttered a whoop and skated toward him. Hen wobbled on his skates an instant, then turned, intent on escape.

"Oh, say, fellows," called Dick, "don't be all the time picking on poor old Hen."

"We'll just wash his face," shouted back one of the pursuers.

Hen knew they meant it, and he was traveling down the ice, now, under full steam.

"Come on, fellows," called Dick, to Greg and to Tom Reade. "We don't want to see Hen abused."

"Why does he get so fresh, then?" demanded Greg, but he started, as did Tom. Dick & Co. were all fleet skaters. They surged to the front of the pursuers, who took it for granted that Dick and his friends were going to aid them, and therefore set up a shout of joy.

Hen Dutcher was traveling with so much effort that he panted hard as he skated.

"Get him, Dick!" sang out Ben Alvord, as Prescott shot ahead of the others.

Hen, looking back, saw Dick gaining on him swiftly, while Greg and Tom were just behind.

"They're mean as all-git-out!" sputtered panting Hen. "Why can't they let a fellow alone? Don't they think I've got as much right to talk as the rest of 'em? Well, I'll show 'em that I have!"

At this moment Dick overtook the fugitive, linking arms with him.

"You let me alone!" snarled Hen. "You're meaner'n poison!"

"Am I?" smiled Dick. "See here, Hen, face about and don't let the fellows bluff you out of a week's growth. Just turn on them. They won't do anything to you."

"If they try it on, I'll fix 'em, no matter what desperate thing I have to do to get square," snarled Hen.

"Oh, cut out all the war talk," Dick advised him gently. "Now, wheel about."

"You lemme alone! I know where I'm going," snapped Hen, making a big effort to break loose from Dick's hold. The effort proved a disastrous one, for Hen tripped himself, slid along for a few feet and then sat down with a jarring bump on the ice. Dick Prescott all but shared the same fate.

"Now, we've got him!" chuckled Ben Alvord, racing in and reaching out for the luckless Dutcher.

The unexpected happened. Hen swung around, as on a pivot,

extending a foot in such a way as to trip Ben and send him down on his own face.

In the gasp of astonishment that followed Hen got upon his feet, gave a swift push with his left skate and was away.

"After him, fellows!" roared Toby Ross. "We'll hold him and let Ben do the face-washing."

Dick, Tom and Greg had shot past the scene. Now they circled and came back, their faces aglow with the fast sport and the keen air.

Hen tried to make for the shore, but got in where the surface of the ice was rough and choppy. Ned Allen and Toby reached out to grasp Hen as they neared him. Young Dutcher made a switching-away movement, and the next instant he had fallen flat on his face. He let out a howl.

"We've got him!" declared Toby, as he and Allen pounced on the prostrate one.

"Yes, but let him alone, fellows," urged Dick, reaching the scene and halting. "Hen may have his faults, but it's time we chose another fellow to pick on for a while."

"We're going to wash his face," insisted Ben Alvord, skating up and looking belligerent. "Don't you interfere, Dick Prescott!"

Hen, making no effort to do more than sit up, was blubbering softly.

"Lemme alone, fellows," he pleaded. "Can't you see I'm hurt?"

Hen had his right mitten off, and was gingerly applying that hand to the narrow stretch of upper lip. There was blood there. Hen, catching only an imperfect view as he gazed down past the end of his nose, was sure that he had been badly injured by his fall.

Some of the other boys set up a yell of laughter.

"Why, you big baby!" blurted Toby. "You've only scratched your lip on the ice."

"A handful of snow will heal it!" asserted Ben Alvord. "Come, get up, bone-head! Come on to your dousing."

"You lemme alone, I tell you!" screamed Dutcher, blubbering. "I've got to go home and get myself attended to."

"Come on, booby!" jeered Alvord, forcing a hand under one of Hen's shoulders and trying to lift him.

"Lemme alone. Can't you see I'm badly hurt?"

"Let Hen alone," broke in Dick quietly.

"He's got to come ashore and have his face washed in the snow," insisted Alvord. "Come, fellows, help me take him there."

"You'd better step back and let him alone, Ben!" spoke Dick, more quietly than before, but there was a sound of command in his voice as he moved over between Hen and Alvord.

"Get out of the way," growled Ben. "This ivory-top has got to have his face washed in the snow."

"And I say you're not going to do it," warned Dick.

H. Irving Hancock

"He's too fresh, Hen is."

"No committee of citizens has asked you to reform any one, Ben," Dick went on good-humoredly. "You've got a few faults of your own that you might remedy, and I guess we all have."

"Come on, fellows, and rush Dutcher," called Ben Alvord. Ross, Allen and others moved as though to help, but Dick was flanked by Tom and Greg. In the distance Dave Darrin could be seen skating back.

"All right, if you fellows insist on it," partly agreed Dick. "But if trouble starts Hen is going to have some backing on his side, too."

"I guess that's right," nodded Tom Reade.

"Now, who's fresh?" challenged Ben Alvord hotly. "You, Dick Prescott."

"Well, if I am," sighed Dick, "I'm ready to take my punishment for it. At all events, I'll look after myself."

"Yah, you will!" growled Ben angrily. "I notice that, just as soon as anything starts, your gang always jump in on the scene!"

"Dick will fight you, all alone, I know, Ben, if you want him to," proposed Dave Darrin, coming slowly into the circle. "But perhaps you don't want to fight Dick. You tried it once before, and got most beautifully pounded."

"Yah!" snarled Ben.

"Well, didn't you?" demanded Dave.

"Yah!" sneered Ben. "See here, Darrin, Prescott may be fresh, but he ain't as bad as you are!"

"So it's I you want to fight with, is it?" laughed Dave. "Come right on to the shore, then, and don't try any bluffing."

But Ben Alvord didn't care about putting up his guard before either of these spirited youngsters of the Central Grammar School. After sputtering a little Ben skated away by himself. Hen got up, after dabbing his upper lip with his handkerchief and finding that the scratch amounted to nothing. No further effort was made to molest Hen.

"Now, when you talk, say something pleasant. Don't talk so disagreeably all the time," advised Prescott in a low tone. "At least, not unless you're really hunting trouble."

"This is the meanest crowd I ever saw," declared Hen Dutcher stiffly. "And you started it all, Dave Darrin, by nick-naming me 'Anvil Chorus!'"

"You're at it again, Hen," sighed Dick. "Why can't you stop saying disagreeable things?"

Toby Ross, who had skated close enough to hear this last, now skated away again to join a crowd of boys a little way off. Toby spoke to them laughingly. Then, over the ice, came a mocking chorus:

"Oh, you Anvil!"

"There, you see," muttered Dutcher angrily, "you've gone and fastened the nickname on me!"

"Anvil! Anvil!" yelled other tormentors.

H. Irving Hancock

"You're all of you about the meanest crowd of fellows I ever saw," grunted Hen, as he started slowly to skate away.

"And that's all the thanks you get, Dick, for trying to use him a bit decently," jeered Greg Holmes.

"Oh, well, I'm sorry for the fellow," muttered Prescott. "Hen is one of those fellows who are never popular with any crowd and can never understand why."

Harry Hazelton and Dan Dalzell now skated up from town and joined their chums. Dick & Co. were at last united.

"Let's try a two-mile swift skate up river, fellows," urged Dick. "Ready? Go!"

Away went the six, moving along over the ice like young human whirlwinds. Dick & Co. were known to be the best skaters of all the Grammar School boys in town.

Dick & Co. will need no introduction to the readers of the first volume in this series, entitled "THE GRAMMAR SCHOOL BOYS OF GRIDLEY." Our readers have met all six of the young men, namely, Dick Prescott, Dave Darrin, Greg Holmes, Dan Dalzell, Tom Reade and Harry Hazelton. It would be hard to find six manlier boys of thirteen—now all of them close to their fourteenth birthdays.

Readers of the previous volume know on what grounds it can be claimed that these six were real leaders of the little Grammar School world of Gridley. Dick & Co. were ardent lovers of all forms of outdoor sports. All were keen for baseball. As runners these six youngsters were just beginning to develop as a result of self-training. The September before Dick Prescott had organized, at the Central Grammar School, a football squad. Things were moving well in this line until delegations came over from the North and South Grammars, to see about organizing a Grammar School football league. The delegates from the two other schools, however, displayed lack of harmony, and the football idea fell through.

Now, however, winter was on in earnest, and Dick & Co. were in their element, for, of all sports, they loved those that went with winter. All six were fearless coasters; no hill was too steep, too long or too dangerous. On the ice Dick & Co. felt all the bounding pulse of life.

This day was the twenty-fourth of December. School had closed in order to give the Gridley youngsters a free hand on the last day before Christmas.

The river had been frozen in fine condition for more than a week. Not more than four inches of snow had fallen, but all the boys knew that the season gave promise of more snow ere long.

As Dick & Co. skated along the number of other skaters became fewer. At last they reached a part of the river where they had the ice all to themselves.

"There's Payson's orchard, Greg," sang out Dave Darrin. "The place where you got grabbed last fall, by Dexter and Driggs, and carried off to be shut up in that cave."

"Say, we ought to hunt up that cave, fellows," called Greg. "Whee! It might make a bully place for a winter camp. Now, that we've got the two weeks and more of holiday vacation, wouldn't it be fine to slip off and camp a few days in that cave?"

"Nothing doing," retorted Tom Reade.

"Why not?" Dan asked.

"You remember that I went off, yesterday after school, on a sleigh ride with Jim Foley?"

"Yes."

"Well, we went by that cave," Tom continued. "Nothing would do but that we stop. Jim had a lantern on the sleigh. We lit the lantern and got into the cave. Whew! We nearly got drowned. I meant to tell you fellows about it, but forgot it."

"How did you come near getting drowned in a cave?" Greg demanded.

"Why, the outlandish place isn't weather-tight," responded Tom. "You know, the flooring slopes slightly upward from the entrance. There are a lot of cracks that rain and snow-water leak through. It was all little rivulets inside the place. Camp? Huh! It'd make a better extra reservoir for the town water-works, that place would!"

"Too bad!" muttered Greg. "I have had a notion that it would be huge fun to camp out in such a place."

"I've got another idea about that," spoke up Dan.

"Fire away!" begged Reade.

"A cousin of mine who visited me last summer told me about the kind of camp he and some of his chums had. It was a sort of manufactured cave. The fellows dug an oblong hole in the ground. Just like a cellar in shape, you know. It was eight feet wide and twelve feet long. When they had it all dug out the fellows laid boards over the hole for a roof. Then they piled dirt back on top of the boards, and on top of the dirt they laid the sods that they first dug up. At a corner in one end the fellows left a square hole in the roof, to use for an entrance. For a door they made a square board cover to fit over the entrance hole. At the upper end of the cave they dug into the dirt wall and made a stove. They dug another hole down from above to connect with it, and that made a dandy stove and chimney. My cousin and his chums used to do a lot of cooking there. Then they laid down more old boards to make a floor, and boarded most of the wall space, too. Last of all, they took up an old table and old chairs, and they had just a dandy camp! Say, fellows, why couldn't we have a camp like that?"

"It would do all right for springtime," declared Tom Reade, "but we couldn't work it in winter."

"Why not?" challenged Dan.

"Not unless, Danny, you want to be the strong man who's going to dig down into the ground through two or three feet of frost."

Dan looked a bit crestfallen.

"Besides," declared Dick thoughtfully, "every time there was a thaw or a big rain the cave you're talking about making would be nothing but a big cistern, half-full of water. But we could dig and fit up such a cave somewhere in the woods in springtime, fellows."

"Only we don't have much vacation in the spring," broke in Greg disappointedly, "and it certainly would be grand to go into camp right after Christmas Day, if we could be warm enough and have enough to eat."

H. Irving Hancock

"It would be great sport," nodded Dick.

"Then let's do it," glowed Greg.

"I suppose you have the camping place all picked out, and permission to use it," smiled Prescott.

"Well, no," admitted Greg. "But why can't we fix up some sort of place?"

"How?" Dave Darrin wanted to know. "If we try going into camp at this time of the year we want, first of all, some place above ground, with enough daylight and sunlight. We want a weather-tight place that we can keep properly warm."

"All of that," agreed Dick.

"Why can't we build a place, out in the woods somewhere?" Greg insisted.

"For one thing," objected Tom Reade quizzically, "there are no leaves at this time of the year."

"What do we want leaves for?" queried Greg.

"To lay on the roof, like shingles."

"Bosh!" snapped Holmes. "We'd build our camp of wood."

"Well, where'll we get the wood?" came from Dave.

"We can carry it from home," proposed Greg.

"No lumber pile in our yard. Is there in yours?" Dave insisted.

"We can use the boards from old boxes and things," went on Greg desperately.

"Oh, excuse me!" mimicked Tom Reade. "I am not camping out in any grocery boxes at this cold time of the year."

"You might go home nights, then," hinted Greg disdainfully.

"The whole camping idea is a great one, if we could only put it through," declared Dick.

"Then let's put it through," pressed Greg Holmes. "Where there's a will there's a way, you know."

"The trouble is that we need a pocketbook more than a will," returned Prescott doubtfully. "It would take lumber to build a winter camp, even if we could prove ourselves good enough carpenters."

"How much money would it take?"

"Well, I don't believe a hundred dollars would go far," declared Reade.

"Make it a thousand, then," laughed Darrin. "We fellows couldn't raise either sum in a year."

"It's too bad," sighed Harry Hazelton. "A good camp, at this time of the year, would be huge fun!"

"Yes; it would," agreed Dick. "I don't see the way now, but we may find it. We can keep on hoping."

"Hey, you boobs!" called a disagreeable voice across the ice.

All of the six Grammar School boys slowed down and turned

around. They found themselves looking at a solitary skater who had slowed down. He was Fred Ripley, son of Lawyer Ripley, one of the wealthy men of the town. Fred was never over polite to those whom he considered as his "inferiors." Besides, young Ripley was now in his freshman year at the Gridley High School. As such, he naturally looked down on mere Grammar School boys, none of whom, perhaps, would ever reach the dignity of "attending High."

"What do you want, Ripley?" called Dick. "Planning to give us a lesson in the art of polite speech?"

"Cut the funny talk," grumbled Fred. "Prescott, did you get a letter from my guv'nor this morning?"

"Why, no; I didn't know your father was in the habit of writing me letters. Anyway, I left home before the mail carrier was due."

"Guv'nor said that was likely to happen," continued Fred. "So he told me, if I saw you fellows on the ice, to say that he wanted to see you."

"All of us?" Dave wanted to know.

"I reckon so. And the guv'nor said it was important, too. You boobs had better crank up your skates and make fast time. Guv'nor won't be at his office late to-day."

"What—" began Dick.

"The guv'nor gave me a message to you fellows, and I've delivered it," cut in Fred airily, as he started to skate away. "That's all I've got to do in the matter. I don't care to stand here all day. Somebody that knew me might come along and catch me talking with you."

"The snob!" muttered Dave indignantly.

"What on earth can the lawyer want of us?" pondered Greg.

"Generally, when a lawyer sends for you, it means trouble," guessed Dalzell.

"Or else some relative has died and left you a lot of money," added Harry Hazelton.

"Well, in any case," replied Dick, "we six fellows haven't the same relative, anywhere, and Fred said his father wanted to see all of us."

"We haven't been doing anything—nothing wrong, anyway," declared Dan virtuously.

"We won't know the answer until we've seen Mr. Ripley," declared Dick. "We'll have to go around there after dinner to-day."

"Why not go now?" proposed Tom Reade. "We haven't anything special to do with our time."

"You fellows haven't much imagination, have you?" laughed Dave, his eyes twinkling mysteriously.

"Have you guessed?" demanded Dick Prescott.

"Well, it's only a guess, of course, and it may be a wild one."

"Out with it!" ordered Tom Reade sharply.

"You know, fellows," Dave continued, "that we did some service for Mrs. Dexter last fall, and that she tried to reward us. Now that she's gone away to parts unknown, perhaps you also know that Lawyer Ripley is managing her money affairs these days."

"Then—" gasped Greg.

"Why, fellows, now that Mrs. Dexter is away, and we can't stop her, and as to-morrow will be Christmas, why, perhaps—"

Not one single member of Dick & Co. was at all lacking in imagination now!

"Why, do you think—"

"I wonder if—"

"Fellows," hinted Dick Prescott dryly, and in a tone that hid the excitement going on within him, "it won't take us long to skate back to Gridley!"

CHAPTER II

DICK & CO. FIND CAUSE FOR GLEE

Lawyer Ripley was one of the important men of the little city of Gridley. His law practice, which he did not now follow on account of the need of an income, put him in touch with all the wealthier people of the place.

In manner the lawyer was rather severe and austere. He was a good deal of an aristocrat. While he did not seek to repel people, he had little of the knack of drawing people to him in democratic fashion.

"Come in!" he called, in answer to the knock that Dick gave on the door.

As the boys entered they saw the lawyer pausing beside his coat rack.

"I am afraid we have gotten along a little too late, sir," apologized Dick Prescott.

"I can spare you two or three minutes," said the lawyer, turning and going back to his desk.

"Your son said you wished to see us," Prescott continued.

H. Irving Hancock

"Yes," said the lawyer, pulling a drawer in his desk open and glancing inside. "Late yesterday afternoon I received a letter from my client, Mrs. Dexter, who directed me to hand you each a new ten-dollar bill, with her best wishes for a Merry Christmas added."

"I am afraid that Mrs. Dexter intends that as a reward for what we were able to do for her last fall," cried Dick, flushing. "We tried to tell her, at the time, that we didn't want any reward and that we wouldn't feel comfortable in taking one."

"Nothing was said in Mrs. Dexter's letter about a reward," replied the lawyer dryly. "She directed me to hand you the banknotes in place of Christmas cards. I suppose you young gentlemen have no objection to receiving Christmas cards?"

Lawyer Ripley took out several banknotes. One of these he now held out to Prescott.

Dick flushed again, looked embarrassed, then reached out his hand slowly and took the money.

"Will you send Mrs. Dexter our thanks, sir, and tell her that we enjoyed the cards very much?"

"Especially the pictures on them," added Dan Dalzell, as he received his banknote.

"I will send all your messages," nodded the lawyer, as he continued the distribution.

"Say—whoop!" suddenly exploded Greg Holmes.

"What's the matter—yours counterfeit?" laughed Dan.

"Say, fellows," Greg went on, "we were wishing we had the funds to build some sort of a camp. We can do it, now, can't we?"

"What kind of camp?" inquired Lawyer Ripley, looking mildly interested. "And for what would you use a camp?"

"Why, for camping, I suppose," confessed Greg.

"You wouldn't live in a tent, at this time of the year, would you?"

"If we had to," assented young Holmes. "What we were talking about was building some kind of a shack in the woods somewhere."

"Rather a bad time of the year for building operations," smiled Lawyer Ripley dryly.

"But this wouldn't be so very much of an operation, sir," urged Greg. "Now that we've sixty dollars between us, we ought to be able to buy enough lumber to put up quite a shanty."

"Yes; and probably have enough money left to pay for the teaming of the lumber a few miles," agreed the man of law. "But there wouldn't be enough to pay the carpenters."

"We might be able to build a small shack ourselves," proposed Tom Reade.

"Why, so you might," admitted the lawyer, half smiling. "However, any task that is worth doing is much better done by one used to that kind of work. When do you want to go camping?"

"Why, right after to-morrow, Christmas," replied Dick. "We could stay in the woods, if our parents let us go, until about the end of the present vacation."

"It would take you at least that length of time to build the shack, I should think," suggested the lawyer. "Until you had it built you might have to wrap up in the snow at night for your sleep. And, then, when you had it all built, you would discover that the shack didn't belong to you, but to the owner of the land on which you built it. He could order you away from the shack if he were so disposed."

"I hadn't thought of that," admitted Greg, looking crestfallen.

"I'm afraid we won't camp," spoke up Harry Hazelton.

"The greatest difficulty," suggested the lawyer, "would be getting the consent of your parents to any such madcap scheme as going off into the woods to camp, day after day, in mid-winter."

"There might be some difficulty about that, sir," replied Prescott. "But now it looks as though the one really big problem would be to get a camp on the money that we now have, and to be ready to go into it in season during this school vacation."

"That would really be but a very slight difficulty," rejoined the lawyer.

"I wish I could see how you make that out, sir."

"Why, as it happens, in the property that Mrs. Dexter's grandfather left her there's the strip called Hobson's woods, you know. The forest is a pretty big affair. In fact, it's what's generally called wild country. But there are a thousand acres of the woods, worth about four dollars an acre, that now belong to Mrs. Dexter. She authorized me to find a buyer for that bit of the forest, but it seems to be out of the question. Now, on Mrs. Dexter's land, in about the middle of it, and less than two hundred feet off the main trail, is one of the few real old log cabins left in this part of the United States. The cabin is in pretty good repair, too, I fancy, for Mrs. Dexter's grandfather used to do logging out that way. Later in his life, when he had amassed money, the old gentleman used to go out to that cabin to live for a while, two or three times in every year. The place was in excellent repair when he died. It is still, I imagine."

There was a breathless silence as the lawyer ceased speaking. How the thought of that log cabin, out in the deep forest, appealed to the imaginations of such Grammar School boys as these!

"Well, sir?" asked Greg breathlessly, at last.

"Young men, if your parents should consent to your going on such a wild, madcap picnic in mid-winter, I would let you have the use of that cabin. But you may have the use of the cabin at any other time, as long as the cabin remains in Mrs. Dexter's name, so I would suggest your going in the spring or summer."

"Oh, pshaw!" leaped to Greg Holmes's lips, but he choked back the exclamation. What use would boys have for a log cabin in summer, when there was a chance to use it in mid-winter? Besides, the summer seemed a long way off.

"Is there any water near the cabin, Mr. Ripley?" asked Tom Reade, who possessed a practical head in such matters.

"Yes; a spring, within perhaps twenty or thirty feet of the

doorway," nodded the lawyer. "Inside the cabin is one of the big, old-fashioned fire-places—"

"O-o-oh! A-a-ah!" gasped the youngsters in chorus.

"There are also eight bunks in the place, each with a straw or dry-leaf mattress," continued Mr. Ripley. "There are table and chairs, hand made and of the crudest kind, and some few tools."

"Say, wouldn't that make an ideal camp?" demanded Dick Prescott, turning to his chums, his eyes glowing.

All their faces were flushed with the excitement of the thing. Now that it was so close, and practical, all the boys of Dick & Co. felt a wild desire to be up and away for camp at once.

"And you say we may have the cabin, sir, and the right to cut some firewood in the forest?" Dick asked.

"I said you could, if you had your parents' full and free permission to go," replied Lawyer Ripley. "That, I fancy, is a very different thing."

"But if we get that permission, sir," urged Dick, "and come back and tell you so, then you will let us—"

"If you get home permission, you won't need to come back to me at all," replied Lawyer Ripley, smiling, as he rose. "Just go and help yourselves to the cabin and what few improvements it contains. But I am afraid, boys, you are going to be very much disappointed if you expect that your parents will consent. I think it very unlikely that you'll get any such permission. I will send your thanks to Mrs. Dexter, and will also tell her what I have told you about the use of the camp. As to-morrow will be Christmas, I shall not be back here to-day. If you go camping, boys—which I don't believe you will—don't burn the old cabin down unless you find it necessary in order to keep warm enough."

As Lawyer Ripley now made it plain that he was about to leave, the boys hastily repeated their thanks and left the office.

Not until they got down into the street did any of them feel like speaking.

"Say, fellows, if that isn't the grandest—" suddenly blazed forth Greg.

"It's all right," nodded Tom.

"I'm going camping, if I can get any of you fellows to go with me," announced Dave Darrin.

"If your folks will let you, you mean," interrupted Hazelton.

"They will," Dave contended. "And so will yours, Dick."

"I—I hope so," sighed Dick, his eyes dancing. "I never before in my life wanted to do anything as much as I now want to go camping."

"With the still woods, all snow-covered!" cried Dan enthusiastically.

"And the cold nights, with the great fire roaring up the chimney!" supplied Greg.

"And some hunting!"

"And the jolly fun of cooking our own food!"

H. Irving Hancock

These youngsters, as they hurried along the street, were in grave danger of being lost in the depths of their own excitement.

"Say, I wonder if there'd be any fishing out there—through the ice?" demanded Harry Hazelton.

"There'd be some rabbit hunting, anyway," supplied Dan.

"If we can only get leave to go!" groaned Greg anxiously.

"See here, fellows," muttered Dick, halting suddenly. "We've simply got to get that leave from our parents!"

"But how?" challenged Dan.

"That's what we've got to think out right now. And, by hookey! I believe I have an idea. Fellows, we have ten dollars apiece."

"My mother will say that I must put that in bank," grunted Dan.

"Wait! Of course, with ten dollars apiece, we've got to consult our parents as to how the money is to be spent," Dick went on. "Now, that is a matter that will call for a little diplomacy. Some of what our principal, Old Dut, calls 'finish'—no, 'finesse.'"

"What's that?" Dan wanted to know.

"Oh, it's a Latin or a Greek word, or something of the sort, meaning to put a fine edge on a piece of business," Dick explained tranquilly. "What I mean is this, fellows: Each one of us will go home and show the money to his father—his father only. Then each one of us will ask permission to spend five dollars of the money on a present for his mother, to be given to her to-morrow morning as a surprise. Then we'll ask our dads for leave to use the other five dollars towards provisioning our camp. Fellows, if you go about it the right way, I'm sure you can each get leave for the camping expedition! I feel just about sure on my own account."

"But how about our mothers?" inquired Dan dubiously.

"Don't you think the present will smooth the way with the mothers?" laughed Dave Darrin.

"It ought to," smiled Tom Reade.

"Don't you think we could get our mothers something pretty nice with two dollars apiece?" asked Harry Hazelton speculatively.

"I couldn't get anything nice enough for my mother with two dollars, when I have more money," Dick replied promptly.

Hazelton's money-saving plan was promptly voted down.

"So now," proposed Dick, "all we have to do is to hurry home and hustle! Beat your way to it, fellows!"

"Hurrah!" Greg gasped.

Hurrying along Main Street, through the crowds of Christmas shoppers, the Grammar School boys were on the point of parting, to go their several ways homeward, when they came upon a scene that halted them.

More than two dozen people, mostly women, had gathered around a shabby-looking man who was clutching wildly at a lamp post, and yet seemed in momentary danger of falling.

His lips were thickly covered with foam, his eyes glaring, and the fellow was talking wildly, in low tones, as though to himself.

"Come away and leave him. He's intoxicated," announced one woman shrilly.

"He's not intoxicated," responded another matron indignantly. "There is no odor of liquor about the poor man. And drunken men don't froth at the mouth. This poor fellow is ill—very ill. It must be a fit—maybe epilepsy. Some of you women who have a little more brains and heart than others help me to take this poor fellow to the drug store."

There were willing hands enough, now, among the women. Three or four tried to take hold of the sufferer at once. That victim of an unknown malady clutched and gripped at the good Samaritans as they tried to steer him along the street toward the drug store. To hold him up was all four women could do together, so progress along the street was slow indeed.

"Here comes Dr. Bentley in his auto. Stop him, some one!"

The doctor quickly ran his car in toward the curb and leaped out. A fine man and a busy physician, Dr. Bentley was never too much occupied to stop and help an unfortunate man.

Dr. Bentley's big frame and broad shoulders loomed up in the crowd.

"Let me have the man on one side," urged the doctor. "One of you ladies might help hold him on the other side."

"What's the matter with the man, doctor?" cried several.

"Really, ladies, I can't tell until I've had a chance to examine the man. It may be a fit of some sort. I think likely it is. But we will get him to the drug store first, and into the back room. Then I can examine the poor chap comfortably."

Though seemingly "out of his head," the sufferer succeeded in throwing his arms about a great deal.

Then, suddenly, Dick, who had been following and watching with wide-open eyes, called out lustily:

"Dr. Bentley, your overcoat is open, your chain is hanging with no watch on it, and your scarf pin is gone!"

That announcement electrified the situation. Dr. Bentley glanced down swiftly, then threw one hand up to his necktie.

"My purse is gone from my chatelaine!" cried one of the women who had been helping.

"My purse is gone, too!"

It was amazing to see how quickly the sufferer from the fit galvanized into action. He straightened up suddenly, gave himself a violent wrench and shook himself free of those who had sought to aid him.

With a bound the fellow was off and away. As he sprang he spat from his mouth the piece of soap that had supplied the foam to his lips.

"Catch him, fellows!" yelled Dick.

But only Tom and young Prescott were near enough to the path of flight. Tom Reade leaped valiantly in, but was shoved off and sent spinning by one of the burly fists of the rough.

It was up to Dick to make the catch.

Dick had his skates, strapped together, swinging from his right wrist. He swung the skates back to strike at the fugitive. Ere he could do it the man drove a big, hammer-like fist straight between Dick Prescott's eyes in a way that sent that boy down like a log.

The impact of that blow was heard by all.

CHAPTER III

THE CAMPAIGN TO COAX PARENTS

In another moment the fleeing one had darted around the corner.

Five members of Dick & Co., angry all the way through, were the first to reach that corner.

"There he goes, down the alley-way to the livery stable!" roared Dave Darrin. "After him, fellows!"

But by the time that the five reached the stable yard the fugitive was out of sight. Men hurried up, and a quick search was made of the neighborhood. It was soon certain, however, that the fellow had made good use of his time and had gotten away. Two policemen who were among the latest arrivals on the scene gave it as their opinion that further chase would be worse than useless.

So Dick's chums turned back, to see how their leader had fared.

Dr. Bentley was leaning over the boy, who, white and lifeless, lay at the edge of the sidewalk.

"Take him to the drug store, doctor," urged one of the women.

"He'll revive quicker in the open air, madam," answered the physician.

"Is young Prescott very badly hurt?"

"I can't tell yet," said Dr. Bentley. "There doesn't seem to be any fracture of the bone at the point where he was struck. And the back of his head seems to be sound and whole. I think Master Dick is simply stunned."

Dr. Bentley stepped over to his auto, took out a drug case and selected a vial from it.

"Get me a glass of water, someone, and promptly," he directed.

The water was quickly brought. After pouring a few drops from the vial into it, the medical man supported Dick's head and poured some of the stuff into his mouth.

After a short time Dick opened his eyes.

"Wh-what kicked me?" he asked slowly.

"The fist of that gentleman with soap-made fits," replied the physician dryly. "Take a few deep breaths, Prescott. Now, a little more from the glass. Breathe hard again. There, do you feel as though you'd like to get on your feet?"

"Certainly," Dick replied.

Dr. Bentley helped him to his feet, supporting him and urging him to try to walk a little. At about this time Dave and the others returned at a trot.

"Dick, I guess you saved some of us from losing more in the way of valuables," smiled the medical man grimly. "For one, I'm ashamed of myself. A man who has been practising medicine more than twenty years should know too much to be taken in by sham fits on the part of a thief who plays his trick in order to rob a crowd of Christmas shoppers."

"You think he meant to rob us, then, doctor?" pressed a woman in the crowd.

"That fellow certainly did mean to do it," replied Dr. Bentley with emphasis. "It's an old trick in a crowd—this sort of sham sickness."

"And he got all my Christmas money—every cent of it—and carried it off with him!" wailed one woman, who looked as though she could not afford to lose much money.

"He snatched my locket with the diamond in it!" vengefully exclaimed another woman, exhibiting the broken ends of a neck chain.

"My purse is gone. I had forty-two dollars in it."

"I didn't get off very lightly, ladies," replied Dr. Bentley. "My scarf pin wasn't so extremely valuable, but I feel badly about the watch, and I shall feel worse when I realize its loss more fully. That was my father's watch, and I valued it above money."

"The police ought to catch that scoundrel," declared one of the women losers.

"Of course they ought," cried another. "If they don't catch the thief what good are the police, anyway?"

"I don't care much about their finding him, unless they also find my forty-two dollars on him," mournfully proclaimed another of the losers.

"I am sorry for you, ladies. I don't deserve any sympathy, or very little, for myself. Well, as the scoundrel has gotten away, and as young Prescott is growing stronger, I shall go on my way to other patients who need me."

Dick was still rather dizzy and weak, but Dave's right arm supported him.

"Does your head ache?" inquired Greg.

"Guess," advised Dick dryly.

As the two policemen had given up looking for the fugitive, and had gone back to their posts, the crowd was melting. It was nearly noon, and most people on the streets were moving homeward.

"Guess you won't have a large appetite for the coming meal," observed Tom Reade to Dick. "Whew! What a crack that sounded like when the scoundrel struck you! It must have jarred away some of your appetite."

"I can't tell about that until I try to eat," Dick answered.

"No matter whether you eat much or not, but you want to be sure to ask your mother for two cups of strong coffee with your dinner," advised Darrin, with all the readiness of the amateur physician.

"I guess I'll go home, fellows," announced Dick, as the noon whistles blew. "I advise the rest of you to hustle, too. Remember what you've got to spring on your fathers when you get home. We want to have the whole thing settled when we meet this afternoon. Try to put it through, all of you, won't you?"

"I'm going to see you as far as your door, Dick, old fellow," Dave insisted.

"Oh, I'll be feeling fine in another hour," Dick protested. "It just knocked my senses for a minute or two."

Shortly after one o'clock the chums gathered again on Main Street. Dick now looked as keen as ever, and his eyes were shining.

"It's all settled for me," he announced. "I can go camping."

"So can I," Dave reported with satisfaction.

"Dad almost as good as said I could go," Tom declared. "He'll agree to it by to-night."

"How about you, Dan?" queried Dick.

"I can go—*not*," groaned Dalzell.

"I hope to go," announced Greg. "All I could get out of my father was that he was in a rush, but that he'd talk it over with me to-morrow and let me know what he had to say."

Hazelton admitted that he was in the same plight, as to a delayed decision, but he did not speak as though he were very hopeful of being permitted to go.

"It'll just be a shame if we can't all go," Dave declared

seriously. "It won't be a quarter as much fun unless we have the whole crowd."

"Say, watch that slim, well-dressed fellow with the brown derby," whispered Hazelton. "See him coming along behind the two women. I'm sure I saw him, earlier this morning, talking with the same fit-thrower that bumped Dick."

"Humph! So did I," muttered Dick. "I remember. This slim fellow was with a short, thick-set man with a black moustache."

"Right!" nodded Harry.

"They must all be members of the same gang of thieves, then," flashed Dick. "I've read in the newspapers that the thieves who work the Christmas trade generally go in gangs. By crackey! Did you see that?"

"Yes!" muttered Tom Reade excitedly.

"What?" questioned Greg.

"Why," explained Dick, "Mr. Slim put his hand in a woman's skirt pocket. He slipped a wallet from her pocket to his."

"That's what he did," nodded Tom.

"Come along," urged Dick. "We'll see if we can come across a policeman before Mr. Slim gets all the money in the town."

Falling in by twos the Grammar School boys, full of excitement, trailed after the slim, neatly dressed thief.

Two blocks lower down the boys ran across Policeman Whalen, who, in citizen's clothes, had been turned out to watch for thieves.

In an undertone Dick called attention to the slim fellow, who was still moving along in the moving crowds of shopping women. Whalen cautiously took up the trail, while Dick & Co. fell back somewhat.

Two minutes later Whalen made a sudden leap forward, seizing the suspected young man by the coat collar.

"Stand by, till I shake ye down!" roared the policeman, thrashing the thief about until the slim one's teeth chattered. A small morocco purse fell to the sidewalk.

"Why, that's mine!" cried a woman.

"I know it, ma'am. I saw this spalpeen take it from your pocket," nodded Policeman Whalen. "Come along with me, lad! And ye come, too, ma'am, and claim your pocketbook."

"Oh, I'm so glad you saw him do it," quivered the young woman, her face white from the shock caused by the thought of losing her Christmas money.

"I wouldn't have seen him do it," admitted Whalen honestly, "only Dick Prescott called my attention to the spalpeen."

The prisoner, who realized that he could not twist himself away from the strong clutch of the policeman, scowled at Dick as the young woman thanked him.

A crowd formed in an instant, but Whalen broke up the excitement by starting promptly along with his captive.

Dick & Co. turned and followed a little way. The crowd that kept in the wake of the policeman was soon a dense one.

"You'll be sorry for this, youngster!" growled a low, angry voice just behind Dick.

Like a flash Prescott wheeled. It was not plain, however, who, in all that throng, had spoken to him. But Dick's roving gaze soon made out, several yards away, a man in brown, wearing a gray overcoat. The fellow was marching along with the throng as though he, too, were an idle spectator.

"That's the fit-thrower's other friend," flashed through Dick's mind. "He must have been the fellow who spoke behind me just now, too."

"Oh, let's not go any further," proposed Tom Reade. "We've seen folks arrested before this."

"Come along," said Dick shortly, not caring to explain his reasons just at this moment.

So the chums kept on in the wake of the crowd. A block further on a uniformed policeman stepped forward to have a look at Whalen's prisoner.

"Moll-buzzer," explained Policeman Whalen briefly to his brother of the force. A "moll-buzzer" is a thief who robs women in crowds.

The uniformed policeman fell back and the crowd moved forward, but Dick seized the second policeman's coat sleeve.

"There's another of the gang," whispered Dick, pointing to the black-moustached man in the gray overcoat.

"Are you sure?" demanded officer number two.

"Positive," whispered Dick. "At least, we saw them talking

together early this morning."

At this moment the man in the gray overcoat turned. He saw Dick and the policeman talking in low tones. Without waiting an instant the man in the gray overcoat darted forward, trying to break through the crowd.

"Grab him!" shouted the policeman.

Three or four men moved closer to obey.

"Look out!" yelled some one frantically. "He's got a pistol."

The citizen helpers drew away quickly at that information, but the delay had been enough to enable the policeman to close in on his man. With his locust stick the officer struck down the pistol hand and snatched away the weapon. An instant later two prisoners were marching toward the police station, the second one having been taken only on suspicion.

"Bully for you, Dick Prescott!" cried Grocer Smith, laying a heavy but approving hand across Dick's shoulders.

"Oh, we all recognized the pair," Prescott answered modestly. "They were together this morning, and the fit-thrower was with them."

"You boys will be sorry for making unfounded charges of this sort," called back the black-moustached prisoner angrily. "Wait and see if you're not."

"Cut out the gloom, man!" ordered the uniformed policeman, giving his captive a twist that hurt. "Don't be trying to frighten small boys."

At the station house the crowd hung about outside.

"Going inside, Dick!" asked Dave eagerly.

"No one has asked us to. I guess we'd better wait out here unless we're invited inside."

The young woman, whose pocketbook had been taken, went inside. She identified her property and made a charge against the pick-pocket. Both prisoners again heard the name of Dick Prescott mentioned.

The crowd melted after a little. Later the two prisoners were taken before Justice Lee. Mr. Slim was sent away for six months on the charge of pocket picking. The thick set captive in the gray overcoat, because he could not give a good account of himself, was sentenced to ninety days in the workhouse for vagrancy. Police and court were determined to do all in their power to protect the Christmas shoppers.

* * * * *

"Now, as to our camping plans," Dick resumed, a little later in the afternoon. "You fellows who aren't yet sure that you can get leave to go, will have to keep right on the trail until that permission is given. You can say that some of us are going, and that may help you some at home."

"It may help the rest," suggested Dan Dalzell mournfully, "but nothing will do me any good. I'm dished. No camping out in winter is going to come my way."

"Oh, I wouldn't be too sure," urged Dick. "But, at least, you can be sure you won't go if you don't try some more coaxing."

"Say, you come and do the coaxing yourself to-night, when dad is home," begged Dan.

"I will, if you think it will do any good, Danny," Prescott agreed.

"At any rate, your little speech can't put the matter any further back than it stands right now," Dalzell declared. "And, oh, dear! I do want so badly to go with you fellows! I never wanted anything as much before."

"Say, we'll all go together, early this evening," proposed Dick, his eyes now snapping. "We'll call in a body at the house of each fellow who hasn't yet secured leave to go on the winter camping party. We will all present the case. Perhaps we can put it through for the whole six. If we can't all go there won't be nearly as much fun."

Very soon, indeed, after supper, Dick & Co. were all assembled once more.

"You won't need to go to my house," Tom explained triumphantly. "My father says I can go and he has brought mother around to agree to it."

"Whose house shall we go to first, then?" asked Dick.

"Come to mine," begged Dan woefully.

So to the Dalzell home they went. The boys pleaded their case both with Mr. and Mrs. Dalzell. Neither parent, however, would do more than say that "they would see."

At Greg Holmes's house victory was quickly won, and Greg was happy. Next Dick & Co. went in force to Harry Hazelton's home, where the coaxing was renewed.

"I want to sleep over this scheme, Harry," said Mr. Hazelton finally, "and I think your mother does, too. We don't want to see you miss any good times that you really ought to have, so I think, if the rest are going, we shall probably decide to let you go, too. But I won't say 'yes' to-night. I'll wait and see how the idea strikes me to-morrow."

"Oh, I guess you're fixed, all right, Harry," grunted Dan when the Grammar School boys had filed out of the Hazelton house. "But—oh, poor me!"

"And now, see here, fellows, we want to get around into the stores before we lose any more time," suggested Dick. "We don't want to forget that each fellow is to spend half his money in buying the best present he can get for his mother."

"Do you think it will pay—in my case?" asked Dan dolefully.

"Shame on you, Danny boy!" growled Dave Darrin, giving Dalzell a sturdy shaking.

"Was there ever a time that it didn't pay a fellow to remember his mother whenever he had a chance?" demanded Dick. "If my mother had said 'no' and had stuck to it, I'd be mighty glad over being able to get her a solid Christmas present just the same."

Within another hour the presents had been bought, the crowd sticking together and giving collective advice for the benefit of each individual.

Then Dick went home. Instead of passing through the store, where both his parents were, he took out his key and made for the door that admitted to the living rooms above. Over the knob was tacked a piece of paper. Dick took it off and carried it upstairs with him, where, in the light of the parlor, he read this message, in scrawling print:

"Wait and see if you ain't sorry!"

"This must be from the fit-thrower!" thought young Prescott, with an inward jump.

He was soon to know.

CHAPTER IV

"REMEMBERED"—BY MR. FITS?

Through the night Dick slept as only an active, tired out boy can sleep. If he woke once he had no recollection of it in the morning.

This, too, despite the fact that it was Christmas, and he had all of a boy's natural desire to know what the day was to bring him.

Rat-tat-tat! sounded Mrs. Prescott's soft fist on Dick's bedroom door that morning.

"Wake up, son!" Mrs. Prescott called for the second time.

"I—I'm awake," gasped Dick sleepily.

"Get up, then, son. Have you forgotten that this is Christmas?"

"No'm; I haven't." Dick's feet struck the floor heavily, and he reached out for his clothing. "Merry Christmas, mother! Is dad there?"

"He's out in the kitchen, raking the fire. Don't you hear him?"

"Yes'm. Say, mother, have you seen your presents yet?"

"I found a handsome gold chain from your father on my bureau."

"Was that all you found?"

"Yes."

"Where did you look?" chuckled Dick.

"Why, on the parlor table, as usual, to be sure."

"Better look again, mother," laughed Dick.

By this time he was nearly dressed. He heard Mrs. Prescott going back into the parlor.

"I don't find anything else here for me," Mrs. Prescott called back in a puzzled voice.

"Mother, at this rate, you'll soon be needing specs," called Dick, throwing open his bedroom door and looking out.

"But I don't see anything else for me, Richard," insisted his mother, as the boy entered the parlor.

"Look again, mother. Surely, you—"

Then Dick halted suddenly, staring hard at the table, and at the mantel beyond.

"Why, I left—" he began, and then looked more puzzled. At last he grinned as the solution of the mystery came into his mind.

"It's just one of dad's jokes," he laughed. "Or else dad forgot. I gave it to him last night, to lay on the table after you had gone to bed. You see, mother, this is the first Christmas that I have had money of my own with which to buy you something really nice. I'll ask dad where it is."

"Who's taking my name in vain?" called Mr. Prescott, as he came through the hallway and looked in the parlor. "Merry Christmas, Dick."

"Same to you, sir. But, say, what happened to that little package I handed you for mother?"

"I put it on the table before retiring last night," replied Mr. Prescott. "It must be there—but it isn't, is it?"

"Honest, now, dad, this isn't a joke, is it?"

"Not on my part, anyway," replied the elder Prescott rather blankly.

"Now, I suppose that you're both playing a little joke on me, trying to make me curious and impatient," laughed Dick's mother.

"But where is the package?" demanded Dick, exploring all around. His father lent a helping hand in the search.

"Oh, never mind, Dick, dear," urged his mother. "My surprise is bound to turn up. It couldn't have walked out of these rooms. Look at your own package, my boy."

Dick turned to glance eagerly at a not very large box, against which rested a card bearing his own name. He saw, at a glance, that the box bore the imprint of one of the Gridley jewelers.

"I can guess!" cried Dick. "I know what's in the box!"

"Suppose you made a wrong guess?" laughed his mother teasingly. "Better open it and make sure."

Dick picked up the box with trembling fingers.

"Mighty light, whatever it is," he murmured. Then he took off the cover.

"What's this?" choked Dick. "O-o-o-h!"

For all he saw resting in the box was a slip of white paper on which had been poorly printed, in lead pencil, the words:

"Merry Christmas, Master Butt-in!"

"Some of Dad's fooling," laughed Dick a moment later.

"Not much it isn't," retorted Mr. Prescott, taking a quick step forward. "Let me see that paper."

Dick handed it over, and his father read the words.

"What on earth does this mean?" he demanded. "What we put in that box was your first watch, Dick. A silver-cased watch and a very neat gold-plated chain."

One look at his father and a swift glance at his mother convinced the boy that they had not been parties to any joke. Yet where were the watch and chain?

"Who could have left this slip of paper here?" asked Mrs. Prescott.

"Hardly any one outside of the family," replied Mr. Prescott.

"I don't understand this at all."

"And mother's gift, too?" pondered Dick aloud, growing more puzzled every instant.

"Well, certainly no one else has been in this flat," went on Mrs. Prescott.

But Dick flew first to one parlor window, and then to the other. Next he crossed the parlor in two bounds, dashing to his bedroom. He came back, holding the slip of paper he had taken from the outer door the night before.

"The two slips look as though they had been printed by the same fellow, don't they?" inquired the boy.

"Yes," nodded Mr. Prescott. Dick told him about finding the other slip on the door the evening before.

"But who could play such a mean trick?" insisted Mrs. Prescott.

"The fit-thrower, very likely," Dick answered.

"The fit—what?"

Then Dick hastily recalled to them his adventures of the day before.

"And one parlor window is fastened," Dick went on. "The other has its catch slipped. The fit-thrower must have climbed up in the night, slipped the catch with a thin blade and prowled around in here just to spoil our Christmas."

"It looks that way," nodded Mr. Prescott slowly, his usually calm eyes filled with disappointment. Then he added, to his wife: "My dear, I'm very glad, indeed, that I placed your chain on your bureau last night, instead of leaving it here on the parlor table."

"And poor Dick doesn't get any present!" cried Mrs. Prescott, her eyes filling a bit. "O Dick, this year we thought we'd please you more by putting all the money we could spare into one present, so we got your watch and chain that you've wanted for so long. It's—it's too, too bad!"

Mrs. Prescott, though seldom given to tears, now sank to the sofa, pulled out her handkerchief and gave brief vent to her own great disappointment.

"Never mind, mother; it may turn up all right yet," urged Dick soothingly, as he rested one arm around her waist. "But if Mr. Fits really did break in here and take your present, then I feel as though I'd enjoy trailing him to the end of the earth and seeing him shoved away behind strong bars!"

"It seems almost fantastic," declared Mr. Prescott, "but I'm afraid, Dick, that the scoundrel you've told us about really did break in here on purpose to spoil your Christmas. If he didn't come in person he must have sent someone."

"Oh, well, anyway," protested Dick, trying to stifle his disappointment, both on his mother's account and his own, "probably we'll all live to see more Christmases. But, mother, I'm awfully sorry about the loss of your gift. Dad thought, too, that I had made a fine choice."

"Indeed you did, young man," remarked Mr. Prescott. "You know, my dear, that the last time you went to the opera house it was a gala occasion, and you regretted that you didn't have a really nice fan to carry? Dick remembered that, and he got you a fan. It was a handsome one. I didn't believe that a young boy could have as much taste as our son displayed in choosing that fan. And now—it isn't here!"

Then each tried to cheer the other up, but despite their best efforts it started in as a gloomy Christmas morning. The Prescotts, while not by any means poverty stricken, were yet in very moderate circumstances. Dick knew well enough that his parents would not be able to duplicate his much-wanted Christmas gift, and that he would have to wait until some dim time in the future before he could hope to carry a watch of his own.

So all three went out to the breakfast table. Dick, to do him justice, thought more of his mother's loss than of his own.

"Are you going to the police about this, my dear?" Mrs. Prescott asked her husband presently.

"I could," the elder Prescott replied, "but I don't imagine it would do much good. The stuff that has been taken isn't likely to be restored to us. I doubt if the police would think it even worth any effort. It isn't an important robbery, as crime goes. It was just a little trick of revenge."

"Mr. Fits is revenged all right, then," admitted Dick, with a bitter smile. "Oh, I only hope that I get a fair chance to pay him back one of these near days! But, at any rate, my Christmas isn't going to be spoiled. You have already agreed to my going away on the camping trip to-morrow, and that is going to be more fun for me than two Christmases."

"I'm glad you're looking forward so to enjoying your vacation in the forest," smiled Mrs. Prescott. "It does seem fortunate that you have such a treat at hand to repay you for your disappointment."

Suddenly Dick looked blank for an instant. Laying down his knife he employed his right hand in making a frantic thrust into one of his trousers' pockets. Then he fished up a banknote.

"Thank goodness that is all right," he gasped. "Mr. Fits didn't think to look for that. It's my five dollars left out of Mrs. Dexter's present, and is the money that I'm going to pay my share of the camp expenses with. But, on second thought, I believe I'll drop out of that camping scheme."

"Why?" asked Mr. Prescott, in a rather sharp, queer voice.

"Because this five dollars will fool Mr. Fits in another way. I can go to-morrow and get mother another fan like the first one."

Mr. Prescott's eyes flashed proudly for a moment as he answered, a bit huskily.

"You could do that, of course, young man, but your mother would never forgive you for cheating yourself out of the one pleasure you want most."

"Sometimes," spoke Dick gravely, "there's more fun in doing without a pleasure, when you can find another that is worth more to you."

The tears stood in Mrs. Prescott's eyes. She rose and dropped both arms around her boy.

"If we absolutely needed your money, Dick," she said, "I know how cheerfully you would do without your pleasure for our sakes. But this is a case where your going camping will be worth more to us all than anything else that five dollars would buy. Besides, think how disappointed your friends would be over not having their leader."

"I appreciate your mother's feelings so much, lad," went on Mr. Prescott, "that I forbid you to spend your remaining money on anything for your mother. She has had her greatest happiness in knowing that you spent half of the first considerable sum of money you ever had in buying something for her. That is as far as you can go. Illness alone preventing, Dick, you'll go camping, and you'll pay your full share into the camping fund. Besides, I'm glad to say that the indications are that a much better business year is coming, and that probably we'll soon be able to have all the things within reason that we may want."

So Christmas, if it ran rather shy on presents in the Prescott household, was at least a season of extremely good feeling among three people whose sympathies ran staunchly together.

"The fellows will be waiting to see me," laughed Dick after breakfast. "So, if I haven't anything to show 'em, at least I've got something to tell them that will make their hair stand up. And I wonder if Mr. Fits visited any of their homes last night?"

Laughing, though doubtless he felt quite unlike it, Dick Prescott put on coat and hat and went out into the Gridley streets.

CHAPTER V

DICK TRIES STRATEGY

"Hey! Hear about Dick Prescott?"

"What?"

"His Christmas got 'pinched'!"

"No!"

"Sure."

Rapidly indeed did the news travel about. Dick told it to his own chums first. The news "leaked" and traveled up and down the streets as Gridley boys began to come forth to compare their Christmas experiences.

Just as certainly, too, the news didn't lose any on its rounds. By the time that the yarn had been carried to the further end of Main Street, Dick's holiday losses had mounted up to a total of: A gold watch and chain, a diamond stickpin, a twenty dollar gold piece, a suit of clothes, silver plated racing skates, a camera, a cornet and a host of lesser articles.

"Whee! The Prescotts must have been making money this

year," commented Ben Alvord, when he heard the long list of presents named.

"Say," proposed Dave Darrin indignantly, "we'll hike all over Gridley and just see if we can't run into Mr. Fits somewhere. If we find him we'll jump him all together, and then holler for the police."

Quite a bit of searching the six members of Dick & Co. did that morning, though all without the least success. It presently dawned on these Grammar School boys that Mr. Fits must have left Gridley far behind.

"We'll keep our mind on the camping, anyway," proposed Dick. "We want to start to-morrow morning. We ought to meet at eight o'clock, and then get away together as soon after as we can."

"And hoof it twelve miles?" asked Hazelton.

"No; as we'll have so much stuff to carry, we'll have to pay someone to drive the stuff out there for us. If we have a wagon we may as well ride on it."

"I hope you fellows will all have a good time," suggested Dan Dalzell generously, though his own face still wore a doleful look. For his father and mother had held out against his going. All of the other boys had secured permission.

"It's a shame you can't go, Dan," blazed Dave.

"That's what I think," muttered Dan. "Huh! I've a good mind to run away from home."

"You'd get spanked when you went back," laughed Tom Reade.

"Huh! I ought to run away and never come back," growled Dan.

"Oh, cut that out—do!" urged Dick. "Be a fellow of good sense, Danny. Your father and mother have their own reasons for not wanting you to go."

"Their reasons don't do me any good," uttered Dan resentfully.

"Would it do any good if we all went down to your house and tried coaxing for you?" asked Greg Holmes.

"Not a bit," declared Danny gloomily.

"Say, will you fellows wait here a little while?" begged Dick. "I want to run home a minute. I'll be right back."

"Go ahead," nodded Dave.

Dick started on a trot, for he had a new thought as to a possible way of securing Dan's happiness.

As young Prescott turned a corner and raced homeward, he was espied by a boy on the other side of the street.

"Hey, Dick!" challenged Hen Dutcher gleefully. "What time is it?"

Dick flushed, but wisely made no answer.

"Humph!" muttered Hen to himself. "Just as well his watch did get the run-off. Now Dick Prescott won't be hauling his old timepiece out every two minutes in school to see what time it is."

Dick reached home somewhat out of breath.

"Who's been chasing you?" demanded Mr. Prescott, snatching up a cane that stood in the corner of the parlor. He assumed a ferocious expression, which, with one of as peaceable a disposition as Dick's father possessed, looked more than out of place.

"I haven't got time to joke, dad," objected the boy, dropping into a chair. "But I've got something very particular that I want you to do for me, and it will make Christmas really jolly after all if you can do it."

Then Dick unfolded his plan, while Mr. Prescott looked uneasy.

"Why, Dick, my boy, if Dalzell's parents don't want him to go camping it would look very strange in me to call on them and urge them to exchange their own good judgment for mine. It would look like an impertinence on my part. Dan's father and mother are the very best judges as to whether he should be allowed to go away several days camping. In fact, although I've consented to it, I'm not sure that I have shown the best kind of judgment in the matter."

"Oh, I don't want you to urge the Dalzells very hard, dad. I'm not just asking that. But I think, if you talk it over with them, perhaps—"

"It's a queer bit of business for me," remarked Mr. Prescott.

"But will you go, Dad? Please."

"Yes," agreed Mr. Prescott very reluctantly.

"Can you—can you just as easily go soon, dad?"

"Ye-es. I'll go now. It's such a queer piece of business that I shall be thankful when I have it over with."

"And you'll say the best word you can think of, won't you?"

"If you don't stop soon, young man, I may change my mind and back out altogether."

But Dick, who knew well enough that his father's promise, once given, was never gone back on, thanked him and then danced joyously out into the street again.

"What was the matter, Dick?" asked Tom Reade, curiously, when he rejoined his chums. "Did you forget something?"

"There was something I wanted to talk to dad about," responded Dick evasively.

"What—" began Dan, without an inkling of a true guess.

"Be still, you Danny boy," ordered Dave Darrin bluntly. "The family affairs of the Prescotts should be no concern of yours."

Though, very much to his regret, Dick did not possess a watch, he nevertheless managed to keep very good track of the time. Something more than an hour later he led the fellows around to his own corner. He was just in time to see Mr. Prescott returning.

"You stay here a minute," young Prescott directed, then set off at a run to join his father.

"Did you—did you—" he panted, as he reached his parent.

"Yes," replied the head of the family, a bit stiffly. "I made a

H. Irving Hancock

nuisance of myself over at the Dalzells. I talked and talked. They talked, too, and both Mr. and Mrs. Dalzell asked me if I thought it at all safe to let such a busy little gang of hooligans as you boys go off on such an expedition. All I could say was to point out the fact that I had given you leave. Well, Mr. and Mrs. Dalzell gave their consent to Dan's going. So now I hope you're satisfied."

"Satisfied? Oh, dad, thank you! This is the best Christmas ever. Thank you! Whoop!"

With that young Prescott executed an about-face and went charging back to where he had left his chums.

"Are you crazy?" demanded Dan curiously.

"No; but you'll be, in a minute. Dad went over to see your folks, and they've given in. You're to go with us."

CHAPTER VI

THE LOG CABIN'S TELLTALE HEARTH

"Have we got everything?" demanded Tom Reade anxiously.

"I think so," nodded Dick.

"No one ever yet started off on any big jaunt without forgetting something, you know," Greg explained.

"Well, let every fellow take a look around and see if he can find anything that we ought to have, and haven't," suggested Dick.

Six pairs of eyes did some anxious searching.

It was nearly ten o'clock on the morning after Christmas. Dick & Co. stood in Miller's grocery store, having mounted guard over an extensive supply of groceries, meat and personal belongings. What a stack of stuff there was!

Dick and Dave had been delegated to do the buying. Starting with a capital of thirty dollars, they had expended a little more than nineteen dollars with the butcher and grocer. Joe Miller, the grocer's son, had gone to hitch up a pair of horses to a roomy truck wagon. Their conveyance to camp, some twelve miles distant, was to cost them four dollars, and Miller had made a low price at that. Dave, as the treasurer of the outfit, now had nearly seven dollars left, but of this, four would be required to pay Joe Miller for the return trip.

In addition to food supplies, each of the six boys had brought along underclothing, shirts and an extra pair of shoes. These personal belongings were packed in bags.

Then, besides, each boy had a roll of bedding—a pillow, sheets and old blankets and comforters for each. There were also, either in bedding rolls or in bags, some few toilet articles. There was also a box of old kitchen ware. Tom Reade had brought a Rochester lamp; Greg and Dan had contributed lanterns and Dick a dark lantern.

"I see one thing we haven't got, but ought to have," said Harry Hazelton to Dick.

"What's that?" asked the latter.

"A shotgun. Joe Miller has a good one, and I know he'd lend it to us if we asked him."

"We won't ask him," Dick replied.

"Now, why not? We have money enough so we can afford to buy some shells, and—"

"Harry, did you tell your folks you expected there'd be a shotgun along on this trip?"

"'Course not. I didn't know there would be one."

"Do you think your folks would have let you come if they had thought of such a thing?"

"Maybe not. But they didn't say a word against our having one."

"Harry, if our parents were to hear that we had taken a shotgun along they'd be worried to death," said Dick gravely.

"Humph! We're old enough to manage a gun," remonstrated Hazelton.

"Perhaps we are, but it would worry our home folks just the same. Boys are always believed to be careless with firearms. We don't want any shotgun along, and then we won't have any need to be sorry about it afterwards."

"But there'll be rabbits and other game that we might get."

"Dave has brought his air-rifle, and has plenty of 'pills' for it. And Tom brought along his bow and half a dozen arrows. We can take care of the little game we may see."

"That's right," broke in Dave, who had been listening. "If we were fools enough to take along a shotgun it'd be many a day before we'd get leave to go on another camping jaunt."

So better counsel prevailed, and Joe Miller was not asked to loan his shotgun. In due time Joe drove around to the door of the store, and the work of loading began.

"Hey, you fellows, where are you going?" hailed Ben Alvord, stopping and gaping in wonder.

"Camping," replied Dick with an air of importance.

"Whee! Say, take me along?" coaxed Ben.

Dick hated the task of refusing, but Dave came to his rescue.

"Got five dollars, Ben?"

"Quit your kidding," retorted Alvord.

"That's what each fellow paid to get into this outfit," Dave went on. "We couldn't feed any more fellows unless they contributed their share in cash."

"How long you going to be gone?" asked Ben.

"Maybe two weeks."

"Whee!"

"It will depend somewhat on how long it takes us to eat up our table stuff," laughed Dick.

"My, but you fellows are in luck!"

A few more of the Grammar School fellows happened along. There was much envious talk. There were also several pleas to be taken along, but the mention of the five dollar assessment silenced all such requests.

"All ready!" called out Joe Miller at last. "You youngsters jump on lively, for we've got a long way to go."

With a glad whoop Dick & Co. piled aboard the truck, stowing themselves away as comfortably as might be.

"Giddap!" grumbled Joe at the horses.

"Say!" shouted Ben Alvord as the start was made.

"Well?" answered Dan.

"Who's going to do your cookin'?"

"We are."

"Wow! You won't all live to tell the tale, then. Got any medicines with you?"

"There, I knew we'd forgotten something," declared Tom Reade solemnly. "S'posing any of us should get sick?"

"We'll make up our minds that we're not going to," replied Dave. "Fellows camping out in winter haven't any right to get sick."

"Still, we might. Might have colds, especially," remarked Dick thoughtfully. "Oh, I say, Joe! Haul up, quick!"

Dick was standing up, using his arms to signal an automobile that was coming toward them.

"Well, who's sick?" smiled Dr. Bentley, stopping his auto.

"Doctor, I have six free patients here for you," Dick announced solemnly.

"Good!" laughed the physician. "That's the kind I like best. What are you boys up to?"

"We're going camping, doctor, out in the forest, and may be gone a fortnight. Just this minute it struck us that we hadn't a bit of medicine with us in case any of us got sick. We don't expect to be, of course, but—"

"I see," nodded the doctor, smiling pleasantly. "One thing is sure. If you have a few simple remedies along with you you're less likely to be ill than if you had forgotten to make any preparation. In that case worry might do its share. Now, let me see."

Dr. Bentley reached up a drug case from the bottom of his car.

"Here's a bottle of stuff for colds," he went on, selecting a bottle and writing on the label. "There, the directions are straight. Going to cook for yourselves?"

"Certainly."

"Then indigestion is your most likely trouble." Dr. Bentley began to write on the label of a second bottle. "And here's a little vial, in case any of you get a real fever. Be careful to follow the directions closely."

Then Dr. Bentley took out his prescription book and wrote on two leaves.

"Here's a prescription for a liniment, and something else," he added, tearing out the two pages and passing them to Dick. "You'll notice that I've written on these that the druggist is to give you the goods with all discounts off. That'll make the stuff come cheap, for I don't suppose you're overburdened with wealth on this trip."

"And now, doctor, how much for the stuff you've given us?" asked Dick.

"Giddap," retorted Dr. Bentley, giving his machine a start. "I helped introduce four of you boys to this world, so I'm in a measure responsible for you."

"Stop at the drug store, Joe," Dick called out, as the horses were started.

"Say, wasn't that fine of Dr. Bentley?" glowed Dick, as they rode along.

"Sure," nodded Dan, "but our folks will find it somewhere in their bills, between now and summer."

"Dan, for that," warned Prescott, "we'll wash your face in the first snow that falls out in the woods."

"We surely will," confirmed Tom Reade.

The stop at the drug store was made, whereby the cash capital was lowered by eighty cents. Then Dick & Co. were off in earnest.

So late had the start been made that the boys did not expect to reach their log cabin until after two o'clock. Over Christmas most of the snow had disappeared. There was not enough for good sledding, but just enough to make the going on wheels rather difficult.

Before noon, appetite asserted itself. Fortunately the boys had brought along lunches for use on the road. These were devoured with much relish, Joe Miller, of course, being invited to share with them.

By one o'clock the horses headed into the forest. For the first mile or so there was a fair sort of road, but after that it dwindled down to something more like a trail.

"Isn't this grand, Joe?" exclaimed Greg.

"What?" demanded Joe.

"This great old forest, this silence, this grandeur of solitary nature?"

"It ought to do first rate for lunatics, and such like," answered Joe, gazing with disfavor at the bare trees and desolate looking bushes. "What have you boys been doing that you've got to spend a fortnight away from comfortable livin'?"

"Why, we're doing this for pleasure," said Dan Dalzell.

"Humph!" muttered Joe, and there the matter rested.

It was nearly half past two when the horses were finally hauled up before the log cabin. But now the truck was bare of boys. Dick & Co. had leaped overboard the instant they came in sight of the cabin, and had scampered on before for a look at the place.

"Say, this is great!" cried Greg. "The old cabin looks good and solid, too."

"But how do you get in?" queried Dan, bracing his shoulder against the door and pushing hard. "The place seems to be locked."

More boys tried their shoulders against the door, but it did not yield.

"We'll have to try the windows," proposed Dave. "Hurry and see if they're fastened. This one is."

All the windows proved to be fastened.

"We don't want to break any glass," said Tom Reade ruefully. "We might have a big freeze around here, and then we'd appreciate window glass."

Here was a poser, indeed.

"There doesn't seem to be any keyhole, and yet the door is locked," muttered Dick, studying the door. "Hold on! What's this string for?"

He took hold of a cord that appeared to run through the wooden barrier. Giving the cord a hard pull, Dick once more pushed against the door. It yielded and swung open.

"Hurrah!" sounded the chorus.

"We're bright ones," laughed Dick. "Thought we knew a lot about log cabins, and we clean, plumb forgot the latch-string."

"Let's get inside and get warm," begged Dan.

"Let's get warm by tumbling the things off the wagon," dissented Prescott. "I know Joe is in a big hurry to get started back."

So the stuff was bundled off in rapid order, after which Joe backed his team and swung it around.

"I hope you fellows have a real, nice, loony time!" was Joe's parting salute.

"Now, let's get the stuff inside," urged Dave. This was done with speed, if not with order.

"Now, I'll go out and chop firewood," proposed Dave. "Who'll go with me?"

"Let's all go out and take a look around," suggested Dick. "We want to know all of our surroundings before dark, which isn't a great way off."

"We can't have a fire too soon to suit me," grumbled Dan.

Outside one of the first sights that met their eyes, back of the cabin, was a pile of four foot logs that would have measured five or six cords.

"Now, that's what I call bully," gloated Dalzell. "It won't take us long to have a real fire going in that big chimney-place."

"Let's see what this other little shack is," urged Dick, leading the way to a log shanty some eight feet by ten. Again it was necessary to pull a latch-string, after which the door of the shanty yielded.

"Why, there's a cook stove in here, and a table and a couple of chairs," cried Tom. "This must have been the summer cook house."

"We'll use it for our jail to lock up the bad ones in," jested Dick. "There are no bunks here for sleeping."

"What do you say if we get some of those logs and start a fire in the big cabin?" pleaded Dan. "I'm getting chilled."

The idea prevailed. But the youngsters found snow between the logs, which were tightly frozen in place. After a good deal of work and much panting, Dick and Dave succeeded in freeing one log.

"Huh!" grunted Dan, who had not done any of the work. "Getting these logs is going to be harder work than chopping down young trees."

Whistling, Tom Reade had gone around to the cabin. Now, with a whoop of glee he returned, bearing a crowbar.

"Found this in one corner of the cabin," he explained. "Now, we'll pry logs loose in fast order."

His prediction turned out a good one. Within five minutes more than a dozen of the logs had been loosened and Dick & Co. busied themselves in carrying the logs around and into the cabin.

"Now, Danny Coldfeet, we'll soon have your flame red medicine ready," laughed Dave Darrin jovially. "Get one of the coal oil tins, Danny boy. Greg, tear off some of the paper to stuff under the logs. Hurry! Then I'll lay the fire. Tom, you and Harry bring the logs closer."

Some nearly burned bits of log lay in the broad fireplace under the chimney. Dave bent over to lift these charred bits out. Three or four he tossed back of him. Then suddenly he stiffened up, sticking a finger in his mouth.

"Ouch!" he grunted.

"What's the matter?" asked Tom.

"I burned my finger," sighed Dave.

"Burned your finger—in a dead fire?"

But Dick, stirring the burned bits of wood with his shoe, suddenly lay bare some dull red coals.

"Look-a-here, fellows," hailed Dan in the same moment. "Here's meat and bread, and part of a can of tomatoes on the table. The bread ain't old enough to be mouldy."

"Fellows," announced Dick Prescott, moving about, "there's some one living here—some one besides ourselves!"

H. Irving Hancock

CHAPTER VII

THE PROWLER OF THE NIGHT

The six youngsters stood looking curiously at one another.

"I wonder who it can be?" muttered Dan.

"Some one who has no business here, anyway," returned Tom Reade bluntly.

"I wonder if it's some one who did live here, or some one who thinks he's going to keep on living here?" asked Dave Darrin dryly.

"Just the same, I'd like to know who has been living here," Dick went on. "For that matter, who would want to live here, in the depths of the woods in winter?"

"Well, we do, for one crowd," Greg reminded him.

"Yes; but we're boys with a craze for open air and something different," Prescott maintained. "Now, if men have been living here, the case is different. Men don't care about schoolboy junkets. If the man or men who have been living here are honest, I don't mind. Such men will move on if they find that we're here, and that we alone have the proper authority to live here. But suppose the men are not honest? Or rough characters?"

"It will depend on how many there are of them," responded Dan, with one of his broad grins.

"Why?" challenged Dick. "If we had to fight for the right to live in this cabin, how many do you think we could thrash?"

"Oh, I guess it won't come to that," remarked Tom Reade coolly.

"And I hope it won't come to that, or anything like it," Dick replied.

"But just the same, you're going to be scared until you find out? Is that it?" laughed Harry Hazelton.

Dick flushed, but he answered honestly:

"Until something happens I can't tell whether I'm going to be scared or not. Anyway, perhaps I won't show the greatest amount of fright that is displayed around here."

"Now, you're answered, Harry," muttered Dave in a low voice, his eyes flashing. "No fellow in this crowd has any right to doubt that Dick Prescott is all there with the grit when it's called for."

"Can't a fellow joke?" asked Hazelton.

"But, while all this talk is going on," chattered Dan, "I'm not growing any warmer."

"All lend a hand, and we'll get the fireplace cleaned out and the fire going," urged Dick.

After that they made matters fly. The old ashes and hot embers were taken outside and spread. Logs were laid and coal oil spread over them. A match was touched, flames leaped up in response to the heavy draft of the broad chimney, and the interior of the old cabin seemed ablaze.

"My, but that's going to be plenty hot, and some more," chuckled Dan.

"Who'll chop the ice at the spring and get two buckets of water?" called Dick.

"I will," Harry answered, and departed, Greg going along to help him. In a short time Dick had water boiling in a kettle that hung over the fire.

"I don't suppose anyone cares for coffee?" proposed Dick, glancing about him.

In a very short time the beverage was ready.

"Aren't we going to have something to eat, too?" Dan wanted to know, as the young campers gathered at the table.

"What's the use of spoiling our supper, which is only a couple of hours or so away?" asked Dave sensibly.

Though the coffee was weak, it was hot. The youngsters soon began to warm up, and all became cheery.

"Oh, but this life is going to be great!" sighed Greg exultantly. "Say, fellows, I'm glad I thought of this way of putting in a vacation. Won't the other fellows in town be crazy when they hear what a great time we've had?"

"What I want to know," Harry broke in, "is whether rabbits

really do run in the woods in winter? My mouth is made up for some rabbit stew."

"Maybe we can buy a couple of rabbits, then, from some farmer's son," suggested Dick dryly.

"Buy 'em?" sniffed Hazelton scornfully. "Huh! Next thing we know you'll want some one to come in and do the housework!"

"It would be better done, then, I don't doubt," laughed Dick. "Now, fellows, the clock tells us that it's quarter of four. That means something like an hour more of daylight. I guess we've a few things to do, haven't we?"

"Get supper!" proposed Dan.

"That's one of the things," nodded Dick. "Then there's water to be brought in. In this nipping air I'll bet there's already more ice over the spring. Then we ought to bring in a lot more logs for the fire. It'll be harder work after dark. And some one ought to get potatoes ready to put on over the fire. Then we ought to select our bunks and get bedding in them. After that we want to tidy up this hard dirt floor. Some one will need to wash the cups and saucers, and have 'em ready for supper."

"Let's have some system to it, then," urged Dave. "Dick, you look about and see what's needed. Then set each fellow to his task—and all the rest will take any kicker down to the spring and duck him!"

"Lemme fix the potatoes, then," begged Dan. That being one of the "disagreeable" tasks, no one objected. Dick parceled out the tasks, and things were soon humming. While they were still busy, darkness had settled down. But Greg had filled the lamp and the lantern, and had them going, though the big, red fire filled the whole cabin with light.

"Whee! But this is jolly!" cried Greg, as he stood arranging his bedding in the bunk he had chosen.

"It'll be more like fun to-morrow, though," suggested Dick, "when we can have a whole, daylight day out in the woods. But I think we're all going to be mighty comfortable here."

That was the general feeling. The Grammar School boys found themselves filled with contentment.

"How are the potatoes coming on, Danny?" inquired Tom. "I'm so hungry I can hardly stand up."

"Ready in ten minutes more, I reckon," Dan answered cheerily.

"Bully!"

Greg was cutting bread and getting butter out of a glass jar. Dave had busied himself with opening two tins of meat. They had fresh meat, but the latter was to be used on the morrow when their housekeeping arrangements had been better made. For the present the meat and some other perishable articles of food rested on the ground outdoors, under an overturned box on which three large stones had been placed as weights.

"It's six o'clock," called Dick at last. "Are we going to eat on time?"

"I'm all ready with the potatoes," Dan called back.

Dick once more busied himself with making weak coffee.

Tom and Harry set the dishes on the table with a cheery clatter. Then six fearfully hungry boys sat down to table.

"There's no jam on the table," grunted Harry.

"Oh, wait until we get outside of the solid stuff before we bother with sweets," begged Darrin.

It was nearly seven when the glorious meal was over. As nothing but potatoes and coffee had depended on a cook, nothing went wrong with the meal.

"Now, we can clean up and wash the dishes," proposed Dick Prescott.

"What's that?" demanded Tom Reade belligerently. "Work? Right on top of a supper like that?"

"I guess we do all feel more like taking a nap," laughed Dick. "Well, we'll rest for half an hour and see if we feel more like effort then. What do you say if we all pull our chairs up to the fire?"

"How close to the fire?" asked Dan, screening his eyes with his fingers as he glanced at the blazing logs.

"Oh, not too close for comfort, of course," agreed Dick. "But come on. We can swap stories."

"Will they be anything like the spanking story that good Old Dut told you last September, Dick?" teased Dave.

"Not right away, I guess," smiled Dick. "I don't believe any fellow, after that big supper, feels as if he had energy enough to tell a spanking story. But what kind of stories shall we tell?"

"I'll wait for some one else to start it," yawned Tom, as he took his seat in the semi-circle at a respectful distance from the blaze.

"Who else is going to be a quitter or a loafer?" inquired Dave scornfully.

There was a pause. No one appeared to have a story that he wanted to try out on such a critical audience.

At last Dick remarked thoughtfully:

"As the man on the clubhouse steps said—"

Then he paused, as if he had forgotten the matter.

"Well," insisted Greg presently, "what did the man on the clubhouse steps say?"

"Eh?" inquired Dick, gazing at him with mock blankness.

"What did the man on the clubhouse steps say?" repeated Greg.

"Oh—er—that is—it's really a secret," Dick replied provokingly.

"Now, see here, none of that!" growled Tom.

"Eh?" demanded Dan, awaking from a light doze, with a start and a subdued snore.

"Dick Prescott, you tell us what the man on the clubhouse steps said!" ordered Tom.

"But I've just told you that it's a secret."

"None of that, now!"

"But I can't tell secrets!" pleaded Dick.

"It isn't a secret at all. It's a good story, and you've got to let it come out. We need a good one to get us started."

All now joined in the demand, but Dick shook his head protestingly.

"Honestly, fellows, it wouldn't be right for me to tell secrets," he insisted.

The inner bar that locked the door by night had been dropped into place ere the boys sat down to supper. But now Harry rose, went over to the door and raised the bar.

"Fellows," he called back, "give Dick Prescott just one more swift chance to tell us what the man on the clubhouse steps said. If he won't, then grab him and fire him out into the night until he knocks on the door and promises to be good."

Tom, Greg and Dave made a laughing bolt for their young leader.

"Some one's pulling the latch-string from outside," reported Harry Hazelton, too startled, for the moment, to let the bar fall. But Tom wheeled like a flash, leaped forward and dropped the bar back into place.

"It's the fellow, or fellows, who have been living here before we came," whispered Dan in a half-scared voice.

CHAPTER VIII

WORMING THE TRUTH FROM A WHINER

"Let me in—quick!" demanded a voice.

"Move on!" ordered Dave.

"Whoever they are, they can break in through the windows, at any rate," muttered Harry Hazelton, in a voice that was just a trifle unsteady.

"We have legal right to occupy this cabin," called Dick through the door. "No one else has any right to be here."

"I know that," answered the voice, "but let me in before I freeze!"

To the amazement of some of the others, Dick Prescott raised the bar and swung the door open.

In came a figure—that of a boy. His cap was pulled down over his ears, and a big tippet obscured most of his face. But Dick grasped him by the shoulder as the youngster started to enter, followed by a heavy swirl of snow.

"What in the world are you doing here, Hen Dutcher?"

Dick demanded.

"Yes! What are you doing here?" chorused the rest.

"Lemme get near the fire?" begged Hen, in a choking, sobbing voice. "I'm nearly frozen."

"Don't shut that door yet," called Dan, moving forward. "We didn't know it was snowing. I want to see if it's a big snow."

"You bet it is," chattered Hen. "It's a blizzard, and I don't care how soon that door is shut."

"You're not giving orders here, remember," retorted Dan crisply, as he went to the open doorway. The others, too, crowded to the doorway. It certainly was a big snow. The flakes were of the largest size, and coming down thickly to the tune of a moaning wind.

"It wasn't snowing at dark, and now there are at least four inches," cried Greg.

"Five inches," hazarded Dave.

"How many, Dick?"

"Say, are you fellows going to freeze me to death?" called Hen Dutcher, his teeth chattering. He was facing the fire, roasting in front, but with chills running down his spine.

"Close the door, fellows. We can't see much to-night at any rate, and we'll see the whole storm in the morning," proposed Dick. "We don't want to see Hen freeze to death."

"Nobody invited him here!"

Dick turned, wondering who had made that remark, but he could not make up his mind.

"Take off your coat, Hen, and have some hot coffee. We have some left, and it will warm you," Dick went on, after the door had been closed and barred.

"I'll have supper and the whole thing," declared Hen promptly. "Don't you fellows expect to feed your visitors?"

"We'll feed you," Dick agreed, "though we had made no plans for visitors and didn't expect any."

Hen had some difficulty in getting off his coat.

"Are you as stiff as that?" asked Prescott, going to the other fellow's assistance.

"I tell you, I'm just about frozen to death," moaned Hen. "My, how cold it came on, just after dark! The wind began to howl, and I could feel the ice forming on my chin every time I breathed. I thought sure I was going to freeze to death in the woods. I'd about given up when I saw your lights."

"How long has it been snowing?" Dave asked.

"Don't you fellows know?" Hen demanded.

"No; we were in here, getting supper and then eating it. We didn't know that it had even started to snow."

"It wasn't snowing at dark, but it began some time after," replied Hen, as he took the chair Dick offered and sank into it before the warming glow.

"Don't get too close to the fire until you thaw out a bit,"

advised Dick. "If you do you'll feel it more."

"I feel it now," groaned Hen, beginning to moan. "My hands are frozen stiff."

They weren't really frozen, though the hands had been badly nipped. It was twenty minutes before Hen Dutcher cared to move over to the table. Even then he complained severely of the "stinging" in his hands, feet and chin.

"I'm going out," proposed Dave, reaching for his cap and coat. "I'm going to see for myself just how cold it is."

No one offered to accompany Darrin. He paused, outside, to tap on one of the window panes. Two minutes after that he was back, pounding for admittance.

"Br-r-r-r!" Dave greeted his comrades, as he stepped inside. "Say, I don't want any more of being out to-night. I'll bet it's away down below zero. And how the wind howls and cuts!"

It took Hen Dutcher, after he got started, considerable time to eat his fill. In the meantime the others, restrained by a sense of what was due from hosts, held back their curiosity.

"There, I don't believe I could eat another mouthful," declared Dutcher, at last, pushing back from the table.

"Now, Hen," invited Dick, "come over to the fire and tell us how you came to be here."

"Why, I just naturally was hereabouts," declared Hen evasively.

"That won't quite do," replied Dick, shaking his head. "What brought you into these woods to-night? Did you expect that we'd invite you in to join us?"

"Nope. Not quite," Hen replied, a crafty look in his eyes.

"Then out with the truth, Hen Dutcher!" broke in Dave.

"I don't have to tell you fellows, do I?"

"Yes, if you want to stay here to-night!" blurted Tom Reade.

"You fellows wouldn't put me out in the cold again!" dared Hen.

"Wouldn't we?" retorted Greg Holmes.

"I just wanted a tramp, and took one," replied Hen sulkily.

"That's too thin!" snapped Dan Dalzell.

"Then you fellows can invent your own story," offered Hen.

"Out with him, fellows!" called Harry Hazelton, making a dive for Hen.

"Don't you dare!" blustered Dutcher tremulously.

"Out with Hen, if he doesn't tell the truth, and the whole of it," advised Tom Reade.

"Dick, you ain't going to let these fellows do anything of the sort, are you?" quavered Hen. "Why, I'd die if I had to be put out into the storm again."

"Why can't you tell us the truth, Hen?" asked Dick quietly, fixing a searching gaze on Dutcher. Then, with a sudden flash of inspiration, Dick added, "Who was out this way with you?"

"No one," Hen replied.

"Don't tell us that," warned young Prescott. "Who were the other fellows in the crowd?"

"I tell you I came alone," Hen insisted, with rising color, as he shifted under Dick's steady gaze. "Fred and—"

"Fred—who?" cross-examined Dick.

"Nobody," Dutcher answered, his eyes on the floor.

Dick thought a moment before a great light dawned on him.

"So, Hen Dutcher, Fred Ripley and some of his crowd knew we were coming out here, and so they came along, too, and you with 'em, eh?"

"I tell you I wasn't with 'em," protested Dutcher.

"You walked all the way?"

"Most of the way."

"And how did Fred Ripley and his crowd come?"

"On a wagon, and—"

Here Hen Dutcher paused suddenly.

"I came alone," he bellowed wrathfully. "There weren't any other fellows."

"Don't you call Ripley a fellow?" pressed Dick. "You said that he and his crowd came on a wagon. So they're going to play pranks on us, are they?"

"I don't know what you're talking about," protested Hen hoarsely.

Dave, Tom and Greg fastened on Dutcher, dragging him out of his chair. This time Dick did not feel called upon to interfere.

"Now, you tell us all about this queer game!" commanded Dave Darrin, his eyes flashing warningly. "If you don't, we'll shake it out of you; or we'll roll you in the snow until we soak the truth out of you! What do Fred Ripley and his crowd mean to do out here to-night?"

"I—I don't know," gasped Hen.

"Yes, you do," warned Dave Darrin crisply.

"No, I don't!"

"Hen Dutcher," Dick interrupted firmly, "we are out here to enjoy ourselves, and we don't propose to be interfered with. We have a right to be here, and no one else has. We've wormed it out of you that Fred Ripley and some other fellows have come out here to torment us. Fred Ripley has no right to come here and play mean tricks on us."

"Who gave you the right to be here?" demanded Hen sullenly. "Wasn't it Fred Ripley's father?"

"Yes; but that gives Fred no right to be mean in the matter, and Lawyer Ripley would be the first to say so, if I went and told him."

"And then you'd be 'Sneak Prescott,'" taunted Hen.

"I didn't say I was going to tell Fred's father," Dick

answered, his color rising, "and I haven't any thought of it, either. Any fellow of anywhere near my own size who calls me a sneak can have his answer—two of them," Dick went on, displaying his fists. "You know that well enough, Hen Dutcher. You're one of our own crowd—that is, you go to the Central Grammar with us, and yet you've joined in with some High School boys to bother us and spoil our fun. Who's the sneak, Hen? Who will the fellows at the Central Grammar call the sneak when they hear about this?"

Hen began to look decidedly uneasy. He was well aware what the Grammar School boys in Gridley did to one of their own number who was voted a sneak.

"I—I didn't mean any harm," muttered Hen, almost whimpering.

"See here," demanded Dick, another idea coming to him, "how much did Fred Ripley pay you to help work against us."

"He didn't pay me nothing," young Dutcher protested ungrammatically.

"How much did he agree to pay you, then? Come—out with it!" insisted Dick.

Hen saw the other chums pressing about him threateningly, so he almost blubbered:

"Said he'd give me a dollar if I did the trick right."

"So there was a trick?" cried Dick quickly; then added ironically: "Hen, you ought never to tell lies. You don't do it skilfully. You let out the truth, despite yourself. You've admitted that you've been hired to work against us—to help

H. Irving Hancock

spoil our peace and comfort. Now, you've got to tell us all the rest of it, or you'll have to take the consequences!"

"Say, don't be mean with a feller!" pleaded Dutcher, ready to snivel.

"We're not mean with you," Dick insisted. "We've a right to protect ourselves, and we're going to do it. Besides, you joined us, and now you've got to be one of us and tell us the whole scheme against us."

"I didn't join you!"

"Do you belong to Fred Ripley's crowd, then? If so, you'd better join that choice gang! Grab hold of him, fellows!"

Dave Darrin and Tom Reade gripped Hen, on either side, with great heartiness. Dan Dalzell ran to unbar the door, after accomplishing which he turned to view what might follow.

"Are you going to tell us, Hen, what Ripley and his crew are plotting against us?" Dick insisted once more.

"They were going to come down here to-night," confessed Hen.

"What were they going to do here?"

"Scare you fellers."

"How?"

"Oh, they've got a lot of sheets, and a frame to rig up on Bert Dodge's shoulders. With the frame above him, and covered with sheets, Bert will make a 'ghost' about ten feet high."

"What else?" pressed Dick.

"Well, they've got a queer kind of whistle they can blow on, and it makes a long, loud moan, or a wail," explained Hen. "Whee! It gave me the creepy shivers the first time I heard it."

"Has Ripley's ghost party got anything else to make the night merry with?" questioned Dick.

"Some kinder colored fire, that they were going to light at quite a distance from here, to give an 'unearthly' glow through the woods."

"What else?"

"Oh, some other things," confessed Hen vaguely. "I can't tell you all that crowd has, for I didn't see it and they wouldn't tell me about it."

"And you turned on Central Grammar boys to help a lot of High School fellows out?" asked Dick in fine scorn.

"Well, I was crazy to have a day or two out here in the woods, and you fellows didn't ask me," protested Hen. "The other crowd did."

"Yes; because they wanted to use you for a tool against us. They wanted to make you their catspaw, Hen Dutcher. Oh, you must feel fine! And the other Central Grammar fellows back in Gridley will be so proud of you!"

"You don't have to tell 'em," urged Hen Dutcher pleadingly.

"No; we don't have to," confirmed Tom Reade. "But we can. And most likely we will. We want to separate the wheat from the chaff at the old Central Gram."

"But, please don't tell 'em," whined Hen.

"We'll see about that," said Dick Prescott. "We won't make a solitary promise. It may depend on how you act, Hen. Now, is there anything more you ought to tell us about what Fred Ripley's crowd intends to do?"

"No-o-o. I don't believe so."

"Who's with Fred Ripley?"

"Bert Dodge."

"Who else?"

Hen named five other young fellows, two of whom were rather worthless High School sophomores.

"And their plan," added Hen, unburdening himself, "was to swoop down here this evening, lay the lines for a first class ghost scare and then see you fellows start running and never stop till you reached Gridley. They've brought some provisions along with them, and they were going to move in here and camp, and laugh, and have a great joke about how the Grammar School kids got cold feet, and—"

"Where are they now?" Dick queried.

"They were going to my Uncle Joel's for a few hours, have supper there and then slip down here. But Uncle Joel's place must be four miles from here, and even he didn't know just where this camp was. So the fellows made me get the best idea I could from my uncle, and then sent me down here to find the place. They'll be mad 'cause I ain't back."

"More likely they'll come, without waiting for you, Hen," observed Dave Darrin grimly.

At this moment the latch-string moved; there was a click of wood against wood as the latch was raised.

"Fellows, it's our ghost party!" whispered Dick, hoarsely. "Stand close by me and sail in when I give the word. We'll do our best to make it hot for the ghost!"

There were varying degrees of bravery shown in that instant. Not one of the Grammar School boys dreamed that they could best Fred Ripley's crew in a rough-and-tumble, but Dick & Co. were all determined to be as "game" as possible.

It was different with Hen Dutcher. He turned pale and shook like a leaf.

CHAPTER IX

THE INTRUDER WHO TRIED TO BE "BOSS"

The heavy door was thrust open—and then the Grammar School boys had the surprise of their lives.

No swarm had invaded their camp. Instead a solitary man, clad in heavy overcoat, and with a cap pulled down over his ears, stamped into the cabin.

In his astonishment and dismay Dick Prescott could not repress the cry of:

"It's Fits—Mr. Fits himself!"

"I see you hain't forgot me!" snarled the fellow, as he slammed the door shut, dropped the bar in the place, and then stood with his back to that barrier.

"See here, you can't stay here," declared Dick, his eyes flashing.

"Can't, eh?" jeered the fellow. "And what's going to stop me?"

"We are. You've no business here."

"And if I don't see fit to go, my young bantam?"

"Then we'll put you out. We're smaller than you are, but there are seven of us—six, I mean," Dick corrected, after a glance at quaking Hen. "You'll find we can take care of you!"

"You kids, eh?" laughed Mr. Fits hoarsely. "Why, if you boys started in to climb over me I'd pick you off and scrunch you, like so many ants. Just try it and see!"

To make his bragging good, Mr. Fits crossed the cabin, helping himself to the chair by the table.

"I see you've got plenty of grub here," the big fellow went on. "I'll bother you to make me some hot coffee and get me the best you have to eat. Step lively, too! Any younker that doesn't move fast enough I'll pick up and swat, and then I'll throw him out in the snow to stay."

Saying which, with a savage snort, Mr. Fits rose and took off his overcoat, tossing it on to the next chair.

"What are you two whispering about?" demanded the rough intruder, eyeing Prescott and Darrin, who were now at the further end of the log cabin.

"Never you mind," Dave retorted tartly.

"Don't give me any impudence, younker!" growled Fits.

"Then don't talk to us," Dick advised.

"I can see that I've got to trim a couple of you," muttered the intruder sourly. "And then, too, I reckon my supper will be coming along faster."

"You'll get no supper here," Dick warned him.

"I won't, hey? Why not, I wonder?" leered the fellow.

"Because we have no poison to mix with the food," Dave retorted.

"I'll have that grub, and some good coffee, set on mighty quick!" growled the visitor. "If that doesn't happen, then I'll run you all out into the snow. You won't last long out there, I warrant you! It's a fearful night."

"Wait!" begged Hen Dutcher. "I'll wait on you, sir."

"No, you won't, Hen," spoke Dick sharply, firmly. "This man doesn't stay here. He's going to leave mighty soon, or he'll wish he had. If you do anything that we can't stand for, Hen, we'll put you outdoors with Mr. Fits."

"You wait on me, boy," ordered Fits gruffly.

"Yes, sir, I—"

"—won't," Dave finished for him snappily. "See here, Hen, you are of no account here. Look out that you don't make yourself too unpopular to be allowed to remain here to-night."

"I see that I've got to teach some of you young cubs a lesson," remarked Fits, rising from the chair.

"Look out that we don't teach you one!" cried Dick. "Watch him, fellows. If Mr. Fits gets too familiar, then sail into him!"

Dick snatched up one hatchet, Greg another. Dan made a

rush for the bow and arrow, fitting a steel tipped arrow to the string. Tom Reade espied the crowbar, and reached it in two bounds. Dave Darrin caught up a stick of firewood, Harry Hazelton following suit.

Hen Dutcher didn't do anything except to slink away to one side of the big room. His bravery didn't go beyond the risk of telling lies.

"If Fits makes a move towards any of us, fellows," commanded Dick, in a tone whose steadiness surprised even young Prescott himself, "then the rest close in on all sides and give this big bully the best you've got."

"I wish there was a hatchet for me," growled Dave, whose eyes were flashing dangerously.

"Take this one," replied Dick, passing over his own hastily snatched-up weapon. Thereupon Prescott fell back for an instant, darting over to a pile of boxes and picking up the air rifle that had been brought along.

"Let's see if this air rifle is working?" pondered Dick aloud. He took quick aim and pressed the trigger.

"You dratted little pirate!" roared Mr. Fits, tensing for a leap forward. "I'll show you—"

"You'll get a lot more, if you don't quit trying to run things here," Dick threatened coolly.

Mr. Fits was waving his right hand aloft. Dick had struck the back of that hand with one of the pellets that the rifle carried in its magazine. The skin wasn't broken on that right hand, but the place stung, just the same, as Mr. Fits well knew.

"Hold on! Give him his supper, if he'll quiet down," urged Dave Darrin, aloud, adding, in a whisper to Dick:

"And while he's eating it I'll try to find the nearest house, and get men to come down here and grab him."

As cautiously as Dave spoke the big fellow heard him.

"Oh, you will, will you?" leered Fits. "Younker, how long do you think you'd live in the storm that's going on outside? It's a blizzard. If you don't believe me, go out and see. I'll wait till you come back."

For answer Dave ran to the door and opened it. A swirl of snow greeted Darrin in the face, and another big swirl of the white fluff blew in on the floor.

"Go right on out in the snow," jeered Mr. Fits. Dave did so, but the other five chums kept their gaze steadily on the unwelcome intruder.

"By Jove, fellows," muttered Dave, as he stamped back into the cabin, "the storm has grown so that I don't believe any of us could get through it for a distance of three or four miles."

"And you see," continued Mr. Fits, "I stay here to-night for one very good reason, if I didn't have any others. It would be plain manslaughter to make me go out into the storm. I'd simply die in it before going a mile."

"The snow is already up over my knees," confirmed Dave Darrin dismally, "and I believe it would be twice as deep before I'd been gone an hour."

"So you see it wouldn't be decent to put me out," jeered the big bully, "even if I were afraid of you younkers and your wild west outfit of toy guns and archery."

Dave closed and barred the door with a grim tightening around the corner of his lips.

"Now I'll trouble you boys to stow your amateur theatrical outfit in a corner and get me a whopping big supper," continued the big fellow, with a grin, as he returned to his former seat. "If you don't—"

He paused impressively, then added:

"If you don't I'll start something moving here that'll show you who's boss. Or, if you feel too respectable to like my company, then you can all put on your overcoats and step outdoors. Maybe you can find your way to some pleasanter place for the night."

"If we could get through the storm," whispered Dick to Dave, "then we might leave him here, and get to help who would come down and grab the scoundrel."

"We'd get along all right at the start," muttered Dave, shaking his head. "But I don't believe, the way the blizzard is coming now, that we'd get more than a mile or so before we'd all lie down in the snow and have to give up the fight. You've no idea, Dick, what a howler and piler this storm is. You ought to go out and try it."

"If you say it can't be done, Dave, I'll take your word. You've as much sand and fight as any of us."

"Supper!" yelled the intruder lustily.

"It's the cook's night off," jeered young Prescott.

H. Irving Hancock

"Oh, it is, hey?" roared the big fellow. "I'll show you."

Jumping to his feet, snatching up the chair on which he had been sitting, and holding it above his head, Mr. Fits charged.

The crisis in the affair had arrived.

CHAPTER X

IN THE GRIP OF THE BIG BLIZZARD

Dick Prescott was squarely in the way. He didn't flinch or dodge, either.

Like a flash he brought the air rifle up for use. But there was nothing wicked in Dick Prescott. Even against such a foe as this big intruder; Dick felt that it would be wrong, wicked, to aim for the face of Mr. Fits.

Instead, Dick aimed for one of the fellow's legs. The little buckshot went where aimed, but through the thick trousers and underwear the little missile had no painful effect.

"Get back, you lunatic!" quivered Dan, in the same instant, drawing the arrow to the head, ready to let drive.

But at that interesting moment another of the Grammar School boys saved the situation. It was Tom Reade, who, just as Mr. Fits started forward, and was still moving, thrust the crowbar between his legs.

Flop! Fits struck the earthen floor rather heavily, the chair flying over the head of Dick Prescott and landing beyond.

"Good chance!" cheered Harry Hazelton, bringing down his stick of firewood with a blow that resounded.

Tom Reade now raised the crowbar once more, standing where he could aim at the fellow's head. Tom was both too generous and too tender hearted to have struck a human being over the head with such an implement, even had Fits given provocation.

"Don't get up, Mr. Fits," warned Dick, still gripping the air rifle. "If you start to do so, it will be the signal for something to happen."

Their nerves tense from the peril of their surroundings, the Grammar School boys, none of whom were cowards at heart, even though they were pretty young, looked positively fierce in the eyes of the prostrate foe.

"You don't any of you dare hit me," he sneered, with an attempt at bluster.

"Don't we?" scowled Dave Darrin. "Then start something— we'll do the rest."

"Get back with that crowbar!" ordered the fellow sullenly. "Put that air rifle down, and drop that bow and arrow."

"Get up and make us," advised Dick Prescott almost placidly. "Now, Mr. Fits, I hope you realize that we're a few too many for you. As we suggested some time ago, we're going to order you out of here—and at once. And we're not going to take any fooling, either."

"But I can't go out," protested the big fellow. "Why, I'd be found frozen to death in the blizzard."

"You won't have to go far," Dick informed him. "You of course know, as well as we do, that there's a little cook shack at the rear of this cabin. There's a stove there, some firewood and two barrels of coal. Now, you're going there—"

"I won't."

"Yes, you are," Prescott asserted. "Unless you want us to beat you up and simply throw you outside into a snowdrift."

"But I'm hungry," protested Mr. Fits. "Also, it's mighty cold lying here."

"Stay right where you are," Dick went on sternly. "Hen, get this fellow's overcoat and throw it on the floor near the door."

Dutcher obeyed, though he seemed to feel decidedly nervous about it.

"Now, Hen," continued the young leader, "go to the food supplies and pick out two tins of corn beef. Got 'em? Also a loaf of bread. Put the stuff on the coat."

This was done.

"Now, Mr. Fits," went on Dick more steadily still, "it would be unwise for you to rise and walk to the door. We'd bother you if you did. But you can crawl over to your coat. Start!"

"What are you trying to do with me?" appealed the recent bully, in a voice that was now full of concern.

"Crawl over to your coat, and we'll tell you the rest of it. If you don't obey, promptly, we'll take the food part away. Start—crawl!"

Mr. Fits obeyed. He appeared wholly to have lost his nerve, but Dick wasn't so sure, for he ordered sharply:

"Watch out, fellows, that he doesn't play 'possum on us. We can't risk that, you know."

Mr. Fits, however, by dint of crawling, reached his overcoat and the food.

"Throw the door open, Dave," desired young Prescott. "Now, Mr. Fits, rise, get your things and hustle around to the shack at the rear. Woe unto you, if you try to turn and come back into this cabin! We won't stand any more of you."

Like one beaten, and knowing it, Fits shambled out into the storm. No one followed him to see that he reached the shack safely. Any man in good health could do far more than perform that feat.

"Shut the door and bar it, please," chattered Dan Dalzell. "Whew, but having that door open has made this place a cold storage plant!"

"Fellows," spoke up Dick, "if this blizzard is to continue, we'll presently freeze to death in here unless we get more firewood while we can."

"All right," grinned Dalzell. "I've a suggestion, and it's a bully one. We'll appoint Hen Dutcher a committee of one on the woodpile. Go out and study your subject, Hen, and bring in your report—I mean, a cord of wood."

"No, you don't!" protested Hen sullenly.

"Get on, now! Beat your way to the wood pile," ordered Tom Reade.

"No slang, please," mocked Dave. "How can a fellow who's going to work hard beat his way, I'd like to know?"

"If you don't think you'd have to beat your way, to reach the wood pile to-night," retorted Tom, "then just go out again and face the wind and storm. Hen, are you going?"

"No, I'm not," snapped Dutcher.

"Then I'm a prophet," declared Reade solemnly. "I can see you and me having trouble."

"I won't go," cried Hen, with an ugly leer. "I know what you want to do. You want to drive me out to that shanty, so that big fellow will jump on me. Go yourself, Mr. Tom Reade."

"It's too hard a storm for any one fellow to bring in the wood alone," interjected Dick. "I'll go, and so will Greg. Hen, you'll come with us."

"No, I won't."

"Yes, you will," Dick informed him. "We've got to leave some of the fellows here, to guard the doorway against Mr. Fits. We three will go and attend to it all, and the rest of the fellows will stay right by the door and see that Mr. Fits, who has been kind enough to go, stays gone. Get on your coat, Greg, and you, too, Hen."

"I'll stay and help guard," proposed Dutcher.

"A bully guard you'd make," jeered Tom. "Into your coat—or else you'll go without one."

Tom took hold of Hen by the collar, propelling him rapidly across the cabin floor. Dick and Greg were slipping rapidly into coats, caps, overshoes and mittens. Dick picked up the crowbar and Greg the lantern. Hen Dutcher, making the gloomy discovery that it must be work or fight, submitted sulkily.

"Don't hold the door open. Open it when we holler," was Dick's parting direction.

"Whew!" muttered Greg, as they stepped outside. The wind blew in their faces as they went around the end of the cabin, nearly taking their breath, while the snow proved, even now, to be above their knees.

"We can do this in the morning just as well," cried Hen, panting in the effort to make himself heard. "Let's go back."

"You try it, if you dare!" challenged Greg, waving the lantern in the other boy's face.

Even with that short distance to go, it took the three youngsters some little time to reach the great pile of logs. Sparks were flying from the chimney-top of the shack, showing that Mr. Fits was preparing to warm himself.

"And that's the way we've treated the fellow who stole mother's Christmas present, and mine," muttered Dick.

At last the boys reached the pile of logs. Dick tackled it bravely with the crowbar. Shortly he had half a dozen logs clear, though he was panting, both from the beating of the storm and from the hard labor he had taken upon himself.

"Get those in," called Dick. "While you're at it I'll pry more loose."

Hen Dutcher picked up the smallest of the logs, starting for the cabin, but Greg caught him by the shoulder.

"See here, Mr. Lazy, if you're going to pick out such easy ones as that, take two at a time."

"I can't," sputtered Hen.

"Then I'll turn you over to Dave Darrin when you get inside."

Hen thereupon picked up another small log, though he pretended to stagger under the double burden. Greg also carried two logs, and he staggered with good reason, for the weight was more than he should have attempted in the deep snow.

In the very little time that had passed the snow seemed to have grown much deeper. By the time the two wood-carriers reached the doorway and were admitted they felt as though they had done an hour's work of the hardest kind.

Dave Darrin stood just inside, booted and capped.

"Good enough," muttered Dave, holding out the air rifle. "Now, Greg, you take this pill-shooter and let me go out for the next wood. We'll send a new fellow every time."

"Then you can take my place, Darrin," proposed Hen readily. "Give me that air rifle."

"Humph!" was all Dave said, as he poked Hen outdoors before him, while Dalzell and Hazelton took the logs and stacked them at the further end of the cabin.

When Dave and Hen returned they carried but a log apiece.

"Dick says each fellow is to take only one log at a time,"

reported Dave. "In that way he thinks we'll last longer and get in more wood. Now, Hen will stay back. Tom, I see you're in your overcoat and ready. Come along with me. Dalzell get ready for the next trip, when I come back with my second log."

"And I'll be ready to help Dick with the crowbar," called out Hazelton, running for his coat.

In this way the Grammar School boys worked rapidly and effectively. Hen was the only one in the crowd who made any objection to the amount of work put upon him. Yet it was an hour and a half, from the start, before Dick would agree that there was wood enough in the cabin.

"For it may snow for three days, and grow colder all the time," Prescott explained. "By morning it may be impossible to get out at all. We don't want to freeze to death."

Truth to tell, the exercise had put all of the Grammar School boys in a fine glow. When, at last, the big lot of wood had been moved and stacked up inside, and they closed the door for good at last, not one of them, despite his hard work in the biting storm, felt really chilled.

"Now, what shall we do?" demanded Dave, his eyes dancing.

"Do you know what time it is?" asked Dick.

"Not far from ten o'clock."

"Yes; past bed time for all of us."

"Do you feel sleepy?" demanded Dave.

"I don't," chorused four or five.

"Let's sit up as late as we like, for once," proposed Greg Holmes. "That's part of the fun of camping."

"Humph! I want to go to bed," gaped Dutcher.

"Well, there's nothing to stop you, Hen," responded Dick pleasantly. "If you're really sleepy our chatting won't keep you awake."

"What bed shall I take?" inquired Hen.

"Any one that you like best. There are eight bunks to only seven fellows, you know."

Hen took a look, finally deciding on one of the two that were nearest to the chimney.

"What blankets shall I use?" he asked.

Dick looked rather blank at that question.

"Use the ones you brought with you," advised Harry Hazelton.

"But I didn't bring any with me," grunted Hen. "Hurry up, for I'm awful sleepy."

"Well, you see, Hen," Dick went on, "we're in something of a fix on the blanket question. Each fellow brought his own, and on a night like this any fellow who lends any of his bedding is bound to catch cold when the fire runs lower and the place gets chilly."

"But I gotter have blankets," whined Dutcher. "I can't freeze, either."

"I'll tell you what you do, Hen," Dick went on. "There are seven overcoats in the crowd. They'll keep you warm enough."

"But there's snow on the coats, or where the snow has melted its water," objected Hen. "I'll tell you what you do. You fellows are going to sit up and you can wait for the coats to dry. Let me have a set of blankets, and some other fellow take the coats when they're dry."

"Well, of all the nerve!" gasped Tom Reade.

"Hen," spoke Dave sternly, "if you can't wait for the coats to dry, then you can sit up in a chair by the fire and throw on another log or two every time you wake up with a chill!"

Finding that he couldn't have his own selfish way, Hen, with much grumbling, arranged the coats on two chairs not far from the fire. When he considered the coats dry enough he crawled into his chosen bunk, grumbling at the coarse tick filled only with dried leaves, and was covered by Dick and Greg. Then the other fellows, after replenishing the fire, sat down to spin stories.

"You tell the first yarn, Dick," proposed Tom.

"Too bad," replied Dick, with a shake of the head. "All I can think of is what the man on the clubhouse steps said."

"And what was that?" demanded Tom Reade, leaning forward.

"I can't tell you, just yet," replied Prescott.

"Go on! Yes, you can."

"No; it's a secret."

"What did the man on the clubhouse steps say?" insisted Dan, jumping up, seizing the crowbar and poising it over Dick's head.

"Put down the curling iron, Danny," laughed Prescott. "What the man on the clubhouse steps said is a secret, and I'm not going to tell you, just yet, anyway. Some day I'll tell you."

So Harry Hazelton started the ball rolling with a story. When it was finished Greg rose and went to the window at the rear of the cabin.

"I can't see any lights in the shack," he called back. "I guess Fits must have turned in."

"I wish we had something better than glass windows between that scoundrel and ourselves," muttered Hazelton. "After we're asleep all Fits would have to do would be to smash a light of glass and jump right in here on us. Chances are that we'd all go on sleeping soundly, too, while he gathered up the tools and then he'd have us by the hair when we did wake up."

"Well, then," proposed Darrin quietly, "we'll fasten the shutters."

"Quit your kidding," begged Dan.

"I'm not kidding."

"But you talk of closing the shutters. There aren't any— worse luck for us."

"Aren't there?" challenged Dave. "Say, didn't you fellows

know that the cabin windows have shutters?"

"Have they?" asked Dick, jumping up.

"Surest thing going," Dave answered. "Come along and I'll show you."

He went over to one of the windows, which was set to run sidewise in top and bottom grooves. On account of the snow and the cold the window stuck a bit, but at last Dave had it open. Then he reached out and tried to pull the outside shutter along in its own grooves.

"Stuck with a bit of ice," Dave reported. "Harry, just bring the kettle."

Darrin then poured some of the boiling water upon the sill, where the shutter stuck. At his next effort the shutter moved. Dave closed it and pegged it so securely that no trick from the outside could loosen that shutter.

This was done in turn to all the other windows. Feeling secure now, the Grammar School boys found themselves drowsy. Between them they fixed up the fire. Then blankets were spread in six bunks, after which the tired youngsters undressed and crawled in under the bedding.

Silence and slumber reigned in that cosy log cabin in the center of the forest that was in the grip of one of the biggest blizzards in years.

CHAPTER XI

SIX BOYS AND ANOTHER IN COLD STORAGE

When the chatter had ceased and the fellows were all dropping off to sleep, the interior of the tight old log cabin was still aglow from the light of the fire. That light was so bright that, one after another, the boys turned over, their faces to the wall.

And then no sound was heard, save the weird howling of the wind outside, with an occasional sputter as a stray gust of snow swept down the broad chimney to the roaring fire. Every Grammar School boy, as he dropped off to sleep, knew that a big blizzard was still in progress.

"I wonder if I'll sleep a wink, for thinking of Mr. Fits, and what he may try to do to us in the night," thought Dan Dalzell, while his lids fell heavily. "If I do sleep, it will be to wake every little while with a start. Well, so much the better. If I wake often I'm likely to hear the scoundrel if he starts anything around here—when he—thinks—we're—so drowsy that we're dead to the world—and—*gullup!*"

That last exclamation was a snore. Dan was conscious of waking once, though at what time he did not know. He noted that the fire seemed to have burned very low, and that it was almost wholly dark within the cabin. Then he dozed. When he awoke once more he could see no glow whatever from the fire. The lantern that had been left lighted had flickered out. Dan felt oppressed by a sense of something awesome.

"What on earth can the time be?" Dan wondered, now quite wide awake and just slightly uneasy. As he peered about through the dark he made out what looked very much like a narrow ray of daylight through a crack in one of the closed shutters.

"It can't be morning," muttered Dan. "And yet—why is the fire out? We left a bully one going."

Dan had thrown his jacket on to the bunk before retiring. Now, he sat up, reaching for the jacket.

"Gracious but it's cold!" gasped Dan, as the chill struck him.

"Shut up!" growled Dave Darrin's drowsy voice. "Don't wake everybody."

"What's the matter?" chimed in Dick Prescott sleepily.

"It's—it's cold," chattered Dan, as he sank back under the blankets. Here he quickly warmed. And he had gotten what he had looked for, a battered old dollar watch and a box of matches.

"Keep under the clothes and you'll be all right," returned Dick soothingly. "But, my! With that fire out some of the fellows are going to have a cold time getting up and building one in the morning."

Dan's teeth chattered for a minute or two. Then he sat up once more, striking a match and holding up his watch.

Dalzell stared incredulously at the hands and the dial before he tossed the extinguished match to the floor and sank back once more under the blankets.

"S-s-say, do you fellows know what time it is?" shivered Dan.

"What time?" called Dick and Dave softly.

"It's half past nine."

"Nonsense," ridiculed Dave. "It was after ten when we went to bed."

"It's after half past nine—in the morning," retorted Dan impressively.

"Glory, but I believe you're right," ejaculated Prescott. "I can see just a tiny crack of daylight over by one of the shutters."

"It's morning, all right," Dan insisted. "And the fire's out. Wake up, fellows! Who's going to start a new fire?"

"I will," volunteered Tom Reade. "Great Scott! No; I won't, either," he ejaculated, after having thrust his legs out of his bunk preparatory to jumping up. "Oh, don't I wish we could carry a million freight carloads of this cold air back with us! We could make our fortunes selling it to a cold storage company."

"I guess we'll have to call for two volunteers," laughed Dick, after having thrust a foot out. "I'll volunteer, for one. Who'll be the other?"

"Hen Dutcher!" came with wonderful unanimity from the others.

"Not on your life I won't!" retorted Hen with vigor. "I won't freeze myself for any gang of fellows, and that's flat. I'm going to dress by a warm fire when I dress."

"Well," said Dan ruefully, "as I woke all the others up, I guess it's up to me to volunteer. Say when you're ready, Dick."

"Now!" answered Prescott.

"Please don't be so sudden," pleaded Dan. "Give a fellow just a bit of warning. Count three; no, make it ten."

So Dick counted. At ten both he and Dan leaped from their bunks. They were sorry, the instant their feet struck the floor, which seemed at least twenty degrees colder than ice. Both shook and shivered as they pulled on their underclothes, shoes which they did not stop to lace, then shirts, trousers, vests and jackets.

"Br-r-r-r! M-m-m-m—!" was all the sound Dan could make. He was trying to frame words, but his teeth wouldn't stop long enough. Dick made a dive for a lot of excelsior that had come around some of their goods the day before. This he threw into the dead, cold fireplace. Dan, shaking as though with ague, brought a log and laid it across the excelsior. Dick brought some more firewood. In a short time they had it well heaped. Then Dick poured coal oil over the whole, and Dan, with palsied fingers, made three attempts before he could open his match box and strike a match. The temperature in the cabin must have been around zero, for it was twenty below outside that same morning.

At last the lighted match reached the oil soaked excelsior, but before it could ignite, the cold wind that was roaring down the chimney blew it out.

Dick was too cold to talk, but he made a dive for his cap, and held it in place over some of the excelsior, while shaking Dan miserably felt for another match. This time the tiny flame caught in the excelsior.

"It's a g-g-g-g-go!" chattered Dick.

"M-m-m-me for b-b-b-b-bed!" chattered Dan, racing back to his bunk in the starting light of the fire and diving in under the blankets.

But Dick Prescott stuck at his post. He saw the excelsior blaze briskly. Then the flames licked at the oil over the logs. Thirty seconds after that, and the cabin interior was fairly well lighted by the increasing blaze. Dick wouldn't go back to his bunk, but stood with his back as close as he dared to the fire. Yet the cold air was all around him, and, while his back baked the rest of his body was so cold that his teeth continued to play against each other in six eight time.

"Why don't you get back into bed?" called Tom Reade lazily from his warmth under blankets. But Dick stuck it out. When the first logs were a seething mass of ruddy fire Dick, now chattering less, brought more short logs and piled them on in place. The wind, that day, would take all the wood that was fed to the fire. Gradually Dick stopped chattering. At last he even felt comfortable.

"You fellows can get up now just as well as not," he announced.

Dan was the first to try it.

"Something like," he announced. That brought Dave Darrin out. One by one the other fellows followed—all except Hen.

"You don't catch me out of my bunk until breakfast is ready," announced young Dutcher.

Dick wheeled impatiently, at this hint, but Dave Darrin whispered in his ear:

"Let it go at that, Dick. But after breakfast we'll make him wash all the dishes—every one—and spend the rest of the forenoon slicking up around the place. If he refuses—well, we'll know how to bring him to time."

So Hen was ignored for the time being. Dan and Greg busied themselves in the first breakfast preparations. Dick and Dave, presently, went over to one of the windows, forcing it back and tugging at the shutter, which proved to be frozen in place.

"Bring some hot water, Dan, the minute you get it," urged Dick. This was soon ready and a small amount of it was poured around the sill, loosening the shutter, which was shoved back.

"Glory! Look at the storm!" cried Dick. There was a rush after the glass window had been closed.

Never had a prettier snow scene been exposed to view. The snow was still swirling down, while what had fallen was up level with the window.

"It's a good four feet deep, already!" cried Dave.

"And looks as though it would go on snowing for a week," added Tom Reade joyously.

"Fellows," announced Dick, "we're surely snowbound. That's something that we've often dreamed about. Say, wouldn't it be queer if we had a long spell of this sort of thing, and couldn't—simply couldn't—get back to Central Grammar by the time school opens again after the holidays?"

"If the food holds out it'll be fun," assented Tom Reade.

Soon another shutter was opened, admitting more daylight. When they got around to the rear window, and got it open, Dick pointed to the shack in the rear.

"Well, we know that Mr. Fits hasn't been out to-day," Prescott laughed. "Just look at his door. The drifts have piled against it, higher than the door itself."

Snow scenes, however, do not feed any one. So the boys turned back to the kitchen preparations. What if the bacon and eggs didn't look quite neat enough to suit a real house-keeper? The mess tasted good. So did the fried potatoes, made out of the left overs from last night's boiled ones. Coffee, bread and butter and "store pie." No wonder the youngsters, when they were through with breakfast, and in a cabin now warm from one end to the other, felt, as Dick expressed it:

"Say, we're at peace with the whole world, aren't we?" he asked.

"Yes," agreed Dan solemnly. "Mr. Fits is snowed in tight."

"We're even at peace with Hen Dutcher, the miserable shirk," rumbled Tom Reade.

"That reminds me," said Dick, turning. "Hen, it's up to you to wash all the dishes, and to do it tidily, too."

"I won't," retorted Hen defiantly. "I'm no servant to

you fellows."

"Hen," observed Dick, with a light in his eyes that meant business, "it's past the time now for you to tell us what you'll do and what you won't do. We didn't invite you here, and you didn't pay any share of the expenses that we have been under. Accident made you our guest; we didn't really want you here at all. The same accident that makes it necessary for you to stay here for the present has kept away the rest of your crowd—Fred Ripley and his pals. While you stay here you'll do your full share of the work. If you don't, you'll soon wish you had. Now, your first job is to wash and dry the dishes. After that you'll tidy up the cabin. I'll show you what's needed in that line. Get to work!"

Hen had grown meeker during this address, for he saw that the other fellows approved all that their leader was saying.

"All right," he muttered; "I'll do it, but it ain't a square deal. I'm your guest and I ought not to work."

CHAPTER XII

BLIZZARD TOIL AND A MYSTERY

"Our old college chum, Mr. Fits, isn't stirring yet," reported Greg Holmes, after looking out through the rear window that offered the best view of the cook shack at the rear.

"Too bad," muttered Tom Reade, turning away from a front window where he was watching only the steady fall of the flakes. "If he were a neighbor worth having he'd come out and offer to shovel the paths."

"I wonder how cold it is outdoors?" pondered Hazelton aloud.

"Somewhere below zero, certainly," rejoined Tom. "Suppose we call that definite enough?"

"I'd like to get out into this storm," hinted Dave.

"So would I," nodded Dick with energy. "It would be fine to be out in the grandest storm that we've ever seen! Down in Gridley I suppose the folks have the sidewalks cleaned off."

"Don't you believe it," objected Dan Dalzell. "Not in this storm. Horses couldn't get through it to drag a plow, and it

H. Irving Hancock

would take an army of men to shovel the snow away, for the wind will blow the snow back as fast as a fellow gets a few bushelfuls moved."

"Let's try it and see!" proposed Dick, jumping up and going for his overshoes.

"Mean it?" demanded Dave joyously.

"Surely I do."

"Then I'm with you." Dave ran to where his outdoor apparel lay. "Going with us, Tom?"

"It's a bad example to set some of these small boys," gaped Tom with his most venerable air, "but I'm afraid I can't stay inside while you fellows are enjoying yourselves."

Greg, too, hurried to get on his arctic overshoes and his overcoat. Then he pulled his toboggan cap well down over his ears and neck and donned his mittens.

"There are only two snow shovels," announced Dick. "What are the rest of you going to use?"

"Here's the fire shovel," answered Greg, producing it. "That will be good enough for me."

"Get the door open, Dave," called Dick.

Darrin unbarred the door, trying to swing it open. Tom Reade sprang to his aid, for the bottom of the door was frozen to the sill.

"Bring the hot water, Hen," called Reade.

"Get it yourself," grumbled Hen. But when Tom turned, and Hen saw his face, the latter made haste to bring the tea-kettle.

"I'd better pour the water," proposed Tom, taking the kettle. "Dick, you and Dave begin to yank on the door as soon as you see the hot stream trickling on below."

Reade made economical use of the water, yet it took considerable pouring to loosen up the door at the sill.

"Better go slow with that water," warned Dutcher. "It's the last there is in the place."

"Humph!" retorted Tom. "Once we get outside I guess we can dig our way to the spring."

At last the door yielded and swung open. A mass of snow blew in upon them. Dick leaped at the white wall beyond and began plying his shovel vigorously.

"It's light, and can be easily handled," he called back over his shoulder.

So Dave waited until Dick had made a start of three or four feet. Then he moved out beside his chum, while Greg, the iron shovel in hand, stood at hand waiting for the other two to make room enough for him to be able to help them.

Bump! went the door, for those inside, without coats or exercise, felt the cold that rushed into the cabin.

"Where to?" called Dave, for the wind carried their voices off in the howling blast. "To the spring?"

"We'd better," Dick replied, "as we're out of water."

Between the depth of the snow and the fury of the storm the Grammar School boys quickly discovered that they had taken a huge task upon themselves. After more than ten minutes of laborious shoveling all three paused, as by common consent, and looked at the work accomplished. They had gone barely a dozen feet, and under foot, all the way back to the cabin door, the snow was still some two feet deep.

The distance from the door to the spring being some ninety feet, it was plain that more than an hour would be needed for digging the way to the spring.

"What's the use of all this trouble?" shouted Greg. "We can melt snow, anyway."

"Snow water doesn't taste very good," objected Dave Darrin.

"Besides, we don't want to admit ourselves stumped by a little snow," urged Dick. "Come on, fellows; we can make it if we have grit and industry enough. Here goes!"

With that Dick Prescott began to shovel harder than ever, so the two chums added their efforts. Truth to tell, however, ere they had gone another six feet through the big drifts, their backs were aching. They could have progressed more rapidly, but for the fact that the wind blew much of the snow back into the trench they were cutting through the great banks of white stuff.

"Are we going to make it?" asked Dave dubiously at last.

"We've got to," Dick retorted.

"The other fellows ought to come out and help us," proposed Greg.

"That's not a very bad idea, either," Dick agreed, as he started shoveling once more. "Greg, go back and tell them what we want."

Prescott and Darrin went on shoveling, manfully, until Tom, Dan and Harry came wallowing along over what there was of a path and took the shovels.

After that, with twenty minute shifts, the work went along more rapidly, though once in a while one of the shovelers had to go back over the path, digging out where more snow had blown in.

Hen Dutcher was not asked to share in this strenuous work. He had enough to do in the cabin, and this outdoor performance was no work, anyway, for a whiner.

"Get the axe and some of the buckets," called Dick finally, as he, at the head of a shift, reached and located the spring. The water was, of course, covered with a thick armor of ice. Greg moved into position with the axe, striking fast and hard. Dave and Tom, with the snow shovels, moved back over the opened way, keeping it clear in defiance of the gale. As soon as Greg had the ice chopped away sufficiently, Dick, Dan and Harry began to carry water. There was a water barrel in the cabin.

"If we had filled this yesterday we wouldn't have had to work so hard to-day," half grumbled Dan.

"Well, we want to do something, don't we?" retorted Prescott. "What did we come out into the woods for? Just to sit around indoors and eat and sleep?"

With the utmost industry it took a long time for the youngsters to fill the water barrel.

"Now, we've enough for a week, anyway," remarked Dan, as he and Dick poured the last pailfuls into the barrel.

"Perhaps enough for forty eight hours, though we don't want to be too sure," replied Prescott. "We want water enough for cleanliness, for cooking and for drinking. That will be quite a lot, I guess."

The others now came in, for their outdoor exercise had taken up more than two hours of morning time.

"Wood, next, I suppose," remarked Tom, gazing regretfully at the already diminished pile of wood.

"No; there's wood enough to last until to-morrow; probably until the day after," Dave answered.

"But do any of you fellows see the storm stopping?" queried Dick.

"No," Dave and Tom both admitted.

"Then, as there's no telling how long this good old blizzard will last, we'll do well to stack all the wood we can carry into this cabin."

"Why not take a little rest first?" urged Dan. "I'll do my share of the work, all the time, but I'll admit that I'm tired just now."

"We can divide into two shifts, then," suggested Dick. "As I don't feel very tired, I'll get into the first shift. Tom, do you feel plenty strong?"

"Strong?" sniffed young Reade. "Humph! I'm ready, right now, to meet and vanquish the biggest Bermuda onion that you can produce."

Dave had already started for the door. These three leaders of boydom in Gridley began to ply their shovels vigorously, starting from a point in the path already made to the spring. Working through drifts, in some instances more than six feet deep, it was slow work. After twenty minutes they went back to the cabin, Greg, Harry and Dan coming out to take up the work.

Hen Dutcher was still toiling hard, for he had concluded that industry was the only way to save himself unpleasant happenings.

"How soon are you fellows going to knock off and begin to think about dinner?" demanded Hen.

"When we get good enough appetites, I suppose," laughed Dick.

"Appetites?" sniffed Dutcher. "Huh! I could eat one side of a beef critter, right now."

"Go out in the snow and help one of the fellows, then," advised Tom dryly. "After that you'll be able to eat the whole critter."

"But when are you going to eat?" insisted Hen. "It's noon now."

"We'll eat in another hour, I guess, if that suits the crowd," replied Dick.

"I'm ready to eat right now," coaxed Dutcher.

"But you don't belong to the crowd," retorted Dave Darrin

grimly. "Unless you want to put up with bread you'll have to wait until the crowd is ready."

"Potatoes will be the first thing ready for dinner, Hen," observed Prescott mildly. "As you're not doing anything outdoors, you might get busy peeling a big pan of potatoes."

"See here," flared Dutcher, "I told you before that I'm no servant, and—"

But Dick had risen, for the clock informed him that it was time to relieve the shift out in the deep snow.

"Suit yourself, Hen," replied Prescott. "If you don't peel the potatoes, and some one else has to do it, then you won't eat any hot dinner to-day. That's flat."

"Isn't Dick Prescott just a mean bully?" growled Hen to himself, as the "relief" stepped outdoors to resume work.

"See that Hen keeps busy peeling and washing potatoes," Dick advised Greg in passing.

Then the three rested shovelers took up the task. The path was now approaching the cook shack at the rear of the cabin.

"Queer, isn't it," inquired Dave, "that we don't see a blessed thing of Mr. Fits to-day, and that there's no smoke going up his chimney."

"Perhaps he has left these parts," suggested Tom, rather hopefully.

"How could he?" Dave wanted to know.

"Maybe he went last night."

"I doubt if he could get away, even last night, at the hour when we turned him adrift," Darrin contended. "A man might have gone a quarter of a mile, but he couldn't go a whole mile."

"He hasn't been out to-day, at any rate," declared Dick. "There isn't a trace of a track anywhere near the shack."

"Let's dig up to that window and look in," suggested Dave.

This was done. A few minutes later the three boys stood at the window, glancing in at all they could see of the small interior. Beyond the stove and chairs there appeared to be nothing to see.

"Well, our dear friend Fits isn't on the premises—that's certain," remarked Dave Darrin.

Which conclusion might be true, or, again, might not.

CHAPTER XIII

A VISITOR BY THE AIR ROUTE

When the boys awoke next morning the fire was still burning, though there was not enough of it left to prevent a thin layer of ice forming over the surface of the water in the barrel. Tom Reade slipped from his bunk, drawing on shoes and trousers, and quickly placed a few more logs over the embers. A few minutes after that it was warm enough for the rest to slip out of their bunks and dress hurriedly—all except Hen Dutcher.

Greg soon busied himself, tea-kettle in hand, with thawing the ice around the bottoms of the sliding shutters.

"No tracks at the cook shack," announced young Holmes. "And say, fellows, it has stopped snowing."

"Well, for once in my life," smiled Dick, "I think I've seen enough snow. I just wonder how the folks in Gridley are getting through it."

"Oh, they must have the streets broken, after a fashion, and some sort of paths on the main sidewalks," responded Tom Reade judicially.

All were now at the windows, looking out over the scene. At only two of the windows, however, could a level view be obtained; the two others were completely blocked by piled up snow. The rest of the windows could be used for observation purposes when the Grammar School lads placed boxes on which to stand.

"The snow looks soft yet," declared Dave.

"It is soft; you can see that in the way that the wind catches it up in flurries," Dick argued.

"Then we can't get far in it to-day," decided Tom Reade. "We can't travel far over the snow until we have a cold spell for twenty-four hours that will freeze the top of the snow into a hard crust."

"When that crust comes we just will travel," muttered Dave.

"Getting tired of camp?" grinned Dalzell.

"No, Danny Grin; but you forget something."

"What?"

"We've got a duty to perform. As soon as we can get where there's a telephone, we've got to send word to the Gridley folks that Mr. Fits is in these parts."

"But Mr. Fits isn't here," Greg objected.

"That's so," Darrin admitted slowly. "And yet the rascal must be somewhere around, for he couldn't get far in such a blizzard as we've been going through."

"What I'm even more anxious about than Mr. Fits is

telephoning the news to the home folks that we're all safe here, and as snug and comfortable as can be," Dick interposed. "Whee! But our folks must be worried about us. They'll never let us go camping again in winter."

"Oh, I don't know about that," argued Dave. "If we only prove to them that we can weather such a time as this, without sickness or disaster, they'll be ready to believe that we can take care of ourselves anywhere on earth."

"Why, there isn't anything very hard about taking care of ourselves here," Dick continued. "All we have to do is to show a little industry. We've got everything at hand that we could possibly need. But I wish the home folks knew how comfy and happy we are."

"I'd like to see myself out of this," grumbled Hen Dutcher, lying huddled in his bunk under the pile of overcoats. "Say, fellows, is it warm enough for me to get up yet?"

As all of the real boys in the party were already up, none of them thought it necessary to answer Hen, who presently slid out of his bunk and began to dress rapidly.

"What are we going to have to eat this morning, and when?" Hen wanted to know.

"I guess we'll have a light breakfast this morning," hinted Reade.

"Why?" demanded Dutcher, his jaw dropping.

"So we can have a better appetite for the turkey we brought along. Fellows, don't you think we'd better eat that turkey to-day? It may not keep."

"Turkey?" blurted Hen Dutcher, his eyes dancing with anticipated pleasure. "I didn't know you had any grub as fine as that."

"I've been thinking," proposed Prescott, "that we might as well have some of that turkey for breakfast this morning."

"Why, is it already cooked?" cried Hen.

"Oh, no," Dick admitted.

"Then let's have something else for breakfast and keep the turkey until noon," suggested Dutcher. "I can't wait for my breakfast."

"What do you fellows say?" asked Dick, putting it to a vote, but ignoring Hen. "Shall it be turkey for breakfast?"

"Turkey!" solemnly voted five Grammar School boys.

"I call it a shame to treat a fellow like this," grumbled Hen. "To make a fellow wait so long for his breakfast when he's starving to death!"

But none of the others gave any sign that they heard. Dick went to a shelf on which lay many packages of the food they had brought with them two days before. Dick took down a plain little wooden box and stepped to the table.

"Put on about eight eggs, and boil 'em hard, will you, Greg?" Dick asked. "Tom might tackle the coffee-making this morning. Dan and Harry can get potatoes ready."

"But where's the turkey, then?" queried Hen, watching Dick as he opened the box.

"Right here," proclaimed young Prescott, removing the lid.

"Why, that's—that's codfish, salted and dried!" exploded Hen.

"Well, isn't codfish Cape Cod turkey?" demanded Reade, with a grin.

"Is that the only kind of turkey you have with you?" asked Hen.

"The only kind," smiled Dick. "Don't you like codfish, Hen?"

"Not a little bit," grumbled Dutcher.

"Then you can cut out breakfast, and you'll have a fine appetite at noon," offered Dan consolingly.

"It seems to me that you fellows use me as meanly as you know how," flared Hen. "You ought to be ashamed of yourselves."

"We are," Tom assured the grumbler.

Though the codfish should have been soaked over night, Dick accomplished much the same effect by repeatedly scalding it. Then he put it on to cook in boiling water, and next made a flour sauce in the way that his mother had patiently taught him. The hard boiled eggs, after being cooled in cold water, were sliced up and put over the dish when it was ready. This, with potatoes, bread and butter and weak coffee with condensed milk, made a meal that satisfied all hands. Hen didn't like the meal, but he ate more of it than any one else.

"What are we going to do to-day for fun?" Dan wanted to know as breakfast drew to a close.

"Shovel paths and stock up with water and firewood, I guess," smiled Dick.

"Pshaw! I'm sorry it has to be all work, and that we can't have any fun," remarked Harry Hazelton. "I've just been longing to go hunting and get a rabbit for a stew."

"We'll be here for days and days yet," answered Dick. "I guess we'll be able to find plenty of fun before our camping frolic is over."

"It's fun, just being here and living this way," Darrin declared.

Something beat against one of the windows, causing the boys to look around curiously.

"Just a twig blown off from some tree," declared Tom.

"Is it?" floated back from Greg, who had leaped up and was now hurrying toward the window in question. "It's a pigeon —that's what it is. And the poor thing looks perishing, too."

In truth Mr. Pigeon did seem to be about spent. The poor thing huddled against the sash, as if trying to shelter itself from the biting wind and the fine dust of blown snow.

"Bring the tea-kettle, some one," called Greg, and Dick did so.

"Pour the water on so that I can get the window open," Greg directed. "Just enough to soften the ice so that the sash will move back. Be careful not to let any of the hot water scald the pigeon's feet."

Working gently, in order not to alarm the spent bird, Dick

and Greg soon had the window open, and Greg drew in the all but frozen little flyer.

"Say, we can have pigeon stew, or pie, if anyone knows how to make a pie," cried Hen Dutcher.

"You scoundrel!" breathed Greg fiercely. "Your stomach makes a brute of you, Hen Dutcher!"

"Oh, what's the sense of being silly about nothing but just a bird?" insisted Hen.

"I'll fight any fellow who proposes eating this poor little wayfarer," announced Greg.

"Whatcher getting mad about?" snapped Hen. "Pigeons are made just for eating, and we can—"

"Hold this bird, Dan," urged Greg, passing the pigeon to Dalzell and stepping briskly toward Hen, who, alarmed, retreated, protesting:

"Huh! What are you getting red headed about? Can't you stand a joke?"

"I don't like your style of jokes," retorted Greg, stopping the pursuit. "Don't let me hear any more of 'em."

"In fact, Hen," added Tom, "your continued silence would be the finest thing you could do for us."

"See here!" called Dan. "This is one of our own pigeons— right out of dad's cote. This is the speckled one we call 'Tit-bit.'"

"Say, that seems almost like a letter from home, doesn't it?"

asked Dick, his face beaming. "We'll give our friend the best we have. Put the little fellow in a box, in some soft stuff, not too close to the fire, Dan. And I'll start to boil some of the corn meal. That'll make good food for the little chap when he's feeling more like himself."

In less than half an hour Mr. Pigeon was feeling vastly better. He now hopped about the place, using his wings every now and then in a short flight. Dan was the only one who could get near the little creature now. So it was Dalzell who caught the pigeon and fed it its breakfast of corn meal mush when it was ready.

Soon after the pigeon took to flying more and more. He seemed attracted towards the windows, flying straight at them three or four times.

"Your pigeon isn't showing good manners, Dan," teased Tom. "He is showing as plainly as possible that he doesn't like this crowd."

"Most likely it's Hen he objects to," murmured Dalzell, with a grin. "But I'll tell you what I think Tit-bit wants. He's warm, fed and feels as strong as ever. What he wants, now, is to hit up a pace for Gridley and get back into the cote with his mates."

"How long would it take him to get there?" wondered Tom.

"Why, something like ten or twelve minutes, probably," Dan answered.

"Whee! If we could make it that fast we'd be taking frequent trips," sighed Reade.

"I wouldn't make the trip more'n one way. I'd stay in Gridley after I got there," grumbled Hen, but no one paid any heed to him.

"See here," broke in Dick suddenly, "if that pigeon wants to go home, and is able to, why can't we make him take a message for us? I believe we can—if some one at the other end would only see it."

"Dad always looks the birds over when he feeds 'em in the morning," Dan declared.

"Wait until I get a piece of paper," rejoined Prescott, almost breathless from the hold the idea had taken on him. He got the paper, drew out a pencil, and sat down to write, calling off the words as he wrote them:

"To the home folks. We're all here at the cabin, snug as can be, with plenty of water, firewood and food, and having a jolly time. Don't worry about us. We're having a jolly time."

"Tell 'em I'm here," begged Hen Dutcher. "My folks might like to know."

So Dick added that information and signed his name. Next he rolled the paper up into a cylinder.

"Dan, catch that precious bird of yours," begged the young leader. Dalzell presently accomplished that purpose. Dick tied a string around the pigeon's neck, loosely enough not to choke the bird, and yet securely enough so that the noose could not slip off. Then the paper cylinder was made fast to the string.

"Open the window on the side towards Gridley, Greg," called Dick. "When it's open, Dan, you give your pigeon a start."

As Dan let go the bird fluttered from the sill to the snow. Then, after a moment, little Mr. Pigeon spread his wings and soared skyward. Soon the boys had seen the last of the small traveler, still headed in the direction of home.

"Our folks will soon have the news," declared Dan proudly.

"And, oh—hang it!" gasped Dick disgustedly. "I forgot to add even a word about Mr. Fits!"

"Well, he isn't here with us, at any rate," Dave answered.

CHAPTER XIV

THE MYSTERIOUS VOICES OF THE NIGHT

"Wow! Wow-ow-ow-oo-whoo-oo-oo!"

It would be impossible to convey the weird sound in words.

Six boys and a whiner were asleep in their bunks in the log cabin when that awesome sound first smote the air.

Outside the wind had nearly died down. Dick Prescott, the first to waken, felt a cold chill creep down his spine.

"Wow-ow-ow-ow-ow! Whoo-oo-oo-oo-oo!"

"Wh-wh-what is it?" gasped Dan Dalzell, sitting up in his bunk.

"I don't know," Dick admitted.

Again came the fearsome sound, now louder than ever. Dave Darrin and Tom Reade were now awake and startled.

"What on earth can it be?" demanded Tom.

"It must be Fred Ripley's ghost party," suggested Greg.

"Bosh! Fred Ripley would have to be a real ghost before he could get over the deep snow in the woods," Dick retorted.

Once more came the sound, more piercing than ever. Dick leaped from his bunk and began to dress. Dave and Greg followed suit.

"We'll do our best to find out what it is, fellows," Dick promised them.

Hen Dutcher was chattering and half sobbing.

"If I—I ever g-g-get out of this alive," he chattered, "I'll never stick around y-y-y-you fellows again. I was a f-f-f-fool to let you fellows coax me into staying here."

"Get out, then!" retorted Tom Reade half savagely, as he landed on the floor and began to dress. All were soon up except Hen, who, when a more dismal and bloodcurdling wail than ever came along, hid his head under one of the overcoats that covered him.

"It's a wild cat—that's what it is," declared Greg Holmes.

"Only one objection to that idea," returned Dick Prescott. "No one has ever heard of a wild cat in these parts in forty years."

"Then it's some one out perishing in the cold," suggested Dave.

"Whoever might be out in the cold wouldn't have much time to yell like that about it," argued Dick. "A wayfarer, out in the cold and deep snow to-night, would soon lie down and freeze to death."

But now something happened that made the blood of all the listeners run cold.

"Dea-ath sta-a-alks through the for-r-r-rest!" came the wailing chant.

"That must be the Ripley gang," contended Dick.

"But how can it be? How could they get through the deep snow that won't bear 'em?" Tom wanted to know.

"Then what can it be?"

"Mr. Fits," suggested Harry Hazelton.

"But Fits isn't in the shack, or wasn't," Dave argued. "We haven't seen him around, outdoors or in the shack, since the night we ordered him to go there. If Mr. Fits got away from this neighborhood it was simply impossible for him to get back since then."

"A-a-a-all who he-ear my voi-oi-oice shall die-ie within the hou-ou-our!" came the wail once more.

"O-o-o-h! Please don't!" screamed Hen Dutcher, burrowing in under the massed overcoats. "Please spare me! I'll be a good fellow after this!"

"Keep quiet!" ordered Tom, striding over to the bunk and giving Hen three or four vigorous prods. "If you don't we'll throw you outside!"

"But it's just aw-aw-aw-awful!" chattered the terrified Hen.

Truth to tell, none of the boys were feeling at his best, just then. Dick's glance passed the face of the clock, showing the hour to be just midnight.

Had it been possible to travel through the forest, the Grammar School boys would have felt sure that it was Fred Ripley's crew. Then they would have gone forth to see what was up. But feeling sure that they were the only living beings in this part of the forest, it was impossible to account for the awful sounds that came from without. What made the wailing sound still more frightful was the fact that it all seemed a part of the wind that was now rising gradually. And the clearly uttered, sepulchral words made it all real enough. The wind never talks in words.

Again came the wailing, though this time without words.

"I never believed there were such things as real ghosts," declared Harry Hazelton.

"Then you're a fool. Everybody knows that there are ghosts —and they're fine people that do noble work!" proclaimed chattering Hen from under the weight of clothing. He was trying to win the favor of the ghosts.

"If there are any ghosts around here I wish one of 'em would pick you up in a sheet, take you away and drop you in your own home in Gridley," declared Tom, becoming decidedly irritated by this babyish imitation of a boy.

"Oh, please don't say that!" begged Hen piteously. "The ghost might hear you."

"If he does, and takes Tom's advice," hinted Dave, "we'll soon see it happen."

That was enough to send thirteen year old Hen burrowing more frantically than before.

The cabin was warm and bright inside. Dick, while trying to puzzle out the matter to his satisfaction, carried four more logs to the fire, one after another, and placed them.

Not one of the Grammar School boys had any desire to go to bed at that time, save Hen, who wouldn't dare to be anywhere else. In fact, the Dutcher youngster may have wondered whether he could stand on his feet if he slipped out and into his clothes.

One by one the boys found seats. Dan picked up the air rifle and sat with it across his lap.

"Whoever it is that's doing this trick has surely got us going," laughed Dick uneasily.

"He has," affirmed Dave. "I don't believe in ghosts, but, under the circumstances, this thing that's annoying us is more than some creepy. If we could explain it I don't believe we'd let it worry us any. But I suppose human beings are always most afraid of what they cannot understand."

The wailings came at less frequent intervals now, though they continued to be sufficiently awesome. But when the clock showed two minutes before the hour of one in the morning these words came in a blast:

"The hou-ou-our of de-eath is at hand. The Gr-r-rim Rea-capcr is at the doo-oor!"

"Then please, please, please—GO AWAY!" screamed Hen, his teeth clacking a bone solo.

CHAPTER XV

DICK STRIKES A REAL FIND

Then half an hour passed, a quarter-gale of wind making the only sound that came from outside.

"I think that must have been a sailor's ghost," remarked Prescott, at last, "and he got his bearings wrong. He said, half an hour ago, that he was coming in—but he didn't."

"How can you t-t-talk about g-g-g-ghosts like that?" shuddered Dutcher, whose face was still invisible to the others.

"We might as well go to bed," proposed Dave, using one hand to cover an imitation yawn that was intended to urge the others to courage. "Whatever wild spirit was traveling around here has wandered off in some other direction."

"Don't go to bed," pleaded Hen. "I won't have any one to talk to if all you fellows go to sleep."

For answer Tom Reade climbed up into his bunk, though he kept his shirt and trousers on.

"I'll tell you what," offered Dick. "We'll take turns staying up on guard, just in case something real should happen. The fellow who stays up will walk back and forth, to be sure of remaining awake. He'll also see to it that the fire is kept up."

"Who'll take the first watch?" Harry wanted to know.

"Let Hen do it!" came, in the same breath, from Dave, Tom and Greg.

"I—I wouldn't be any good at that," pleaded Dutcher anxiously.

"No," smiled Dick dryly, "I don't believe you would. As I proposed the guard stunt, I'll take the first dose of my own medicine. Later in the night I'll call Dave, and when he's through he'll call Tom. All you fellows pile back into bed and get some sleep."

"You take the air rifle, then," urged Dan, passing it over. As this rather insignificant weapon might possibly be of some use, in the event of more definite trouble, Dick accepted it.

One after another the fellows dropped off to sleep, all except Hen, who lay very still, with heart thumping wildly.

Half an hour after Prescott's tour of guard duty began three wild wails, wordless, smote the air, one after the other. Dave, Tom and Dan awoke.

"It's all right," Dick called to them, softly. "Nothing but noises. Don't be afraid but I'll call you if its needed."

So those who had a chance, dozed off. Hen didn't have any chance; his cowardly soul wasn't made for sleep when there was any danger about.

It was twenty minutes past three when Dick stepped over and nudged Dave gently, next whispering:

"It's about time for you, now. You call Tom at a little after five, and then tell him to call us all at seven o'clock."

Dave hurriedly dressed and took the air rifle from Dick, the latter then getting back into his bunk and soon dropping off in sleep.

"Seven o'clock! All out! Step lively! Change cars for breakfast!" were the next words that Dick Prescott heard.

By the time that the fellows had dressed, in the warm cabin, and had started to pry the shutters back, the first dim promise of daylight was showing in the east. A little later it was broad daylight.

By this time, too, after most of the fellows had slept soundly for hours, the situation seemed altogether different. Even Dutcher slipped out of his bunk and began to dress briskly.

"Say," he grinned, "but you fellows were somewhat scared last night."

"Yes," admitted Dave. "Weren't you?"

"Not a bit," asserted Hen bravely. "Sa-ay—"

He paused, looking around him in wonderment, then demanded tartly:

"What on earth are you fellows laughing at?"

"Laughing just to—to think what boobies we were when we had the brave Hen Dutcher with us to set us a better example," answered Tom Reade sarcastically. "No use in talking, Hen! You're the only fellow in this outfit that has any sand."

"Say, you needn't try to get too funny, now," remarked Hen suspiciously. "You fellows were all so scared that maybe you thought I was as bad as you. But I was only putting it on, just to see how far you'd all go."

"You must have been satisfied, then," returned Dick grimly, "for we surely were uneasy."

Hen blandly took to himself all the credit that was offered him for his "courage," seeing which the Grammar School boys winked slyly one at another, then busied themselves with the tasks of getting breakfast.

"To-day's programme will be more work, I suppose," began Tom, as the lads seated themselves around the table.

"As I see it, it will have to be a day of work," Dick nodded. "For that matter, we're learning that it's no use for boys to go camping, especially in the winter, unless they're willing to work."

"What's to be done first?" Dave wanted to know.

"Well, we'll need more wood, and more water," Prescott replied.

"As it doesn't make much difference which we do first, I'm for getting the wood, if that suits the rest of you. Our path of yesterday is blown over a bit with snow, but we can dig it out again in a little while. And, while we're at that, we may as well dig through to the cook shack again. I want to get a good look in there this time."

"Expect to find Mr. Fits there?" Dave asked.

"Hardly, if we didn't find him there yesterday. But, the more I think about it, the more I feel certain that the noises of last night were in some way connected with the shack."

"I'd like to believe that," muttered Tom. "If that's the case, some of us might sleep in there to-night and catch hold of the noise maker."

"Who'd sleep there?" grimaced Dan.

"Well," responded Reade slowly, "we might let Hen sleep there. He's the bravest of the lot, you know, and so he's just the fellow for the job."

Dutcher choked over the food he was swallowing, and shifted his feet uneasily.

Soon after breakfast was over Dick, Dave and Tom stepped outside with the shovels. Here and there the path had been left fairly clear, though at other points they had to shovel industriously through the new drifts. At last, however, they reached the same window through which they had looked in the day before.

"No sign of any one inside," muttered Dick. "Nor have we seen any signs of fire from the chimney. I can see the stove, now, but there doesn't seem to be any sign of fire in it."

"Let's dig around to the door," proposed Dave, "and go inside."

Accordingly the three bent to the new work. A few minutes later Dick gave a tug at the latch-string and the door swung open.

"It doesn't seem as cold in here as you'd expect to find it," murmured Reade.

"That's because we've just come from where it's a good deal colder," Tom answered.

Dick stepped over to the cook stove, raising a lid.

"Look, fellows; here are a few live coals left here yet."

Dave and Tom joined him, staring at the embers in some astonishment.

"Yet there's no one here, and no tracks in the snow outside," observed Tom. "Say, if the tenant of this place can go over the snow without leaving a trail, it does look rather ghostly, eh?"

"A ghost wouldn't need warmth," Dick retorted promptly.

"Then what's the answer?" challenged Dave.

Dick shook his head, but went to one window after the other.

"No one left or entered here by way of the window," Prescott soon announced. "It struck me that Mr. Fits might have used a window, instead of a door, but if so, there'd be tracks under the windows."

"Mr. Fits hasn't been here at all," Dave replied, with a good deal of positiveness. "When we turned him out into the storm he went somewhere else."

"Then how about the ghostly noises, and the embers in the stove?" Reade wanted to know.

"Ask Dick," prompted Dave.

"I can't tell you," laughed Prescott. "I guess you'll have to ask Hen Dutcher."

"Well, there's no one here but ourselves," Tom went on, as the boys stood staring about the tiny shack. "As far as finding anything here is concerned we may as well go about our task of wood gathering."

"I wish we could get at the bottom of the ghost mystery," muttered Dick wistfully.

"So do I," agreed Reade, "but wishes aren't snow plows, and never were. Fred Ripley and his cronies would be mean enough to come down here and spoil our rest at night, but they'd never be brave enough to face the long trip through the deep snow."

"Well, let's go along and get in the wood," Dick urged. So they went, and more than an hour was spent in carrying logs into the main cabin. Of course Greg, Dan and Harry assisted in this, while Hen was put to his usual morning task of washing dishes and straightening things in the cabin.

For dinner the main dish was a platter of steak, broiled over the wood ashes in the fireplace, where the fire was briefly allowed to burn nearly out.

In the afternoon water hauling was the main occupation, as well as the only sport, for the boys had tried the slight crust on the snow, and had found that it would not bear.

"If it grows colder, and stays so for twenty four hours," declared Dalzell, "then we'll have a crust on all this white stuff that will be strong enough to bear our weight. Then ho for tramping, and for hunting with the air rifle!"

"Huh-m-m-m!" answered Harry. "Rabbits and rabbit stew!"

After the water hauling the Grammar School boys settled themselves for some quiet enjoyment inside the cabin. Dave, Tom, Harry and Greg picked out books and sat down to read near the windows. Dick, on the other hand, elected to rove about the interior of the cabin, looking into odd nooks.

"This water barrel might be a little nearer the fire," proposed Prescott. "Then we wouldn't have to break a crust of ice mornings. Dan, you don't seem to be doing anything. Suppose you come and help move the barrel."

"All right," nodded Dalzell, jumping up. "Where do you want to put it?"

Dick pointed to the spot. As the barrel was two thirds full of water it had to be rolled carefully, to avoid upsetting or spilling. It was no easy task for the two boys.

"Hen, you might come and help us a minute," Dick proposed.

"Whatcher take me for?" Dutcher grumbled. Whereat Tom Reade glanced grimly up from his book to remark:

"Son, when you're spoken to, say 'yes, sir,' and hustle!"

Something in Tom's look induced Hen to move rather promptly. The three boys succeeded in moving the barrel a couple of feet toward the spot desired.

"Hullo," muttered Dick, halting and glancing down at the ground where the barrel had stood since their arrival. "Look at that stone."

The stone lay partly imbedded in the dirt flooring of the cabin. It was a flat, nearly round stone, some fifteen inches in diameter.

"That stone looks like a lid, doesn't it?" Dick asked.

"Cover to a gold mine," sneered Hen.

Dick did not answer, but stepped over, bent and began to pry at the edges of the stone. It did not move easily. Dan brought the crowbar and quietly handed it to his chum.

"What have you got?" demanded Tom, glancing up from his book.

"Don't know yet," Dick laughed.

By the aid of the crowbar Dick pried the stone loose from its setting in the ground.

"There's a hole underneath, anyway," announced Dick. "And—Geewhillikins! Fellows, drop everything but your good names, and come here—quick! Hustle!"

CHAPTER XVI

KEEN ON THE TRAIL OF THE PUZZLE

Breathless with excitement, Dick crouched over the hole in the dirt floor, unwilling to make a move until the other fellows had joined him. That didn't take long.

Hen Dutcher was one of the first to get a glimpse at what had filled Prescott with so much excitement.

"Gracious! It must be Captain Kidd's treasure!" gasped Hen.

"Guess again," replied Tom Reade. "A pirate would be doing a poor business who didn't get a bigger lot of loot than that together."

"But this is a valuable lot of stuff," argued Harry Hazelton, as he took a look.

"I wonder who could have buried it here?" demanded Dan.

"I think I know," nodded Dick. "Now, then, stand back a little and I'll take the stuff out."

The first thing that Prescott drew out of the hole was a paper parcel. This he unwrapped, then gave a whoop of joy.

"The fan I bought mother for Christmas!" he almost shouted.

Something yellowish glinted and caught his eye down in the hole. Dick fished the object out.

"Who's is this?" he queried, holding up a curiously engraved gold watch.

"It looks like Dr. Bentley's," replied Dave Darrin, eying the timepiece. "I saw it often enough when I had diphtheria and he was taking my pulse."

"Yes; it's Dr. Bentley's," glowed Dick. "Won't he be the happy man, though?"

"He will if we manage to get it back to him," assented Tom dryly.

Then a dozen rings, some of them set with gems, and all tied on a string, came to light. There were half a dozen boxes containing jewelry; these boxes undoubtedly had been stolen from women in stores or on the street. A few more rather valuable articles came to light, and then Dick, after opening one jeweler's box and looking inside, emitted a whoop of wild joy.

"This must be the very watch that Fits stole from our parlor —the watch intended for my Christmas present," Prescott cried. "Yes, sir; I'll wager this is my watch."

But at last Dick put it aside with the other loot, and then applied himself to emptying the hole of its few remaining treasures.

"There must be five or six hundred dollars' worth of stuff in the lot," guessed Tom.

"More than that," said Dave.

"So, now, of course, you fellows can guess who hid the stuff here," Dick went on. "It was Mr. Fits who stole Dr. Bentley's watch, and who stole mine, too. So Mr. Fits must have hidden here all this stuff, which represents Mr. Fits's stealings."

"Then all I have to say," observed Tom, "is that if our friend Fits would apply the same amount of industry to honest work he'd be a successful man."

"Until the day before Christmas," Dick continued, "Fits had at least two confederates, whom we helped to put in jail. Probably this stuff was stolen by them all, and then hidden."

"And that was why Fits came back here, and was so anxious to get us out," muttered Dave. "Now, I begin to understand why Fits wanted a hiding place for his plunder even more than for himself. He wanted to leave the stuff in this lonely cabin, and be sure it was safe, until he could find a place where he could sell it. Naturally our coming here upset Mr. Fits's plans, and so bothered him into the bargain."

While the other boys were busy with examining the other pieces of loot, Dick took many an alternate glance at his mother's fan and his own watch.

"I wish we could get this back to Gridley at once, and turn it over to the rightful owners," sighed Greg.

"That wouldn't be the way to go about it, though," Dick responded.

"Why not?"

"Because stolen property, when recovered, has to be turned over to the police first of all. Then, if the thief is caught, the police have the loot as evidence against the thief."

"How long do the police keep the stuff?" demanded Greg.

"Until the thief's trial, if there is one, is over."

"Then, if Fits is caught, Mr. Dick, it may be a long time before you'll have the right to wear your own watch."

"I can wear it now, out here," retorted Prescott, slipping the silver watch into a vest pocket and passing the chain through a buttonhole.

"On second thought, though, I won't. We're not sure that Mr. Fits may not reappear. If he did, and found me wearing a watch, he would understand, and might get fighting mad. If Fits had a fellow rascal or two along with him, they could put up more fight than we boys could take care of. If Fits should come along, and not see any proof that we had found his plunder, he might wait until we are all out of the way before he made any effort to find it. Oh! While I think of it, Greg, I wish you and Hen would take buckets and go to the spring for water."

Dutcher grumbled a bit, though he felt that it wasn't safe to rebel openly. He and Greg were gone some time, for, as usual, the ice over the top of the spring had to be chopped away before the water could be obtained.

So, when Hen came in, after pouring his bucketful into the barrel, he noted that the plunder had vanished.

"What did you do with all the stuff?" Greg demanded curiously.

H. Irving Hancock

"It has vanished," smiled Dick.

Greg said no more, but started outside, followed by Hen. Later in the afternoon Greg was told, in whispers, where the plunder had been hidden anew. Hen, too, demanded this information, but the Grammar School boys thought it best not to enlighten him. If Dutcher were caught alone in the cabin by a fellow like Mr. Fits, Hen wasn't likely to hold out his knowledge against threats, and Fits must not be given another chance at the plunder he had first stolen and then hidden.

Soon after darkness came on supper was ready.

"I wonder if we're going to hear the ghosts to-night," muttered Greg.

"No one knows that," Dick answered. "But I think we'd better keep one fellow on guard when the rest go to bed. The guard can take a two hour trick. He can keep the fire going, and, if anything happens, he can warn the other fellows in turn."

So, at nine o'clock, when the others turned in, Greg, the air rifle in one hand, paced softly up and down the cabin, watching, listening.

But nothing happened during Greg's watch. At eleven he called Tom Reade to relieve him.

Just before midnight the same wailings as on the night before started in again. Within sixty seconds all of the Grammar School boys were awake and listening. The wailings continued, and soon came the same sepulchral warnings of death approaching.

"Queer that the racket doesn't bother us the way it did last night, isn't it?" smiled Dick Prescott.

"It's awful enough!" shivered Hen Dutcher. But he was the only one in the cabin who was much alarmed.

"We went all through it last night, and nothing happened," chuckled Dave. "To-night our address is Missouri, and we'll have to be shown what we're asked to believe."

"Call us promptly, Tom, if anything real happens," Dick urged, and sank back in his bedding to compose himself for more sleep. Soon Reade's watch was a lonely one, for most of his companions were either snoring or breathing heavily.

"Whoever got this trick up will have to think of something newer and more 'scary,'" thought Reade, as he paced the floor.

"Well, you fellows might as well wake up," called Dick, after what seemed to Greg like an interval of possibly five minutes. Greg was the only boy, beside Dutcher, who hadn't been called in the night for a share in the watch duty.

"Say, I thought you didn't go on guard until five o'clock, Dick," remarked Greg drowsily.

"I didn't, but it's seven, now," Dick laughed. "It'll be broad daylight in a few minutes more. Move! Get a hustle on!"

Hen Dutcher, though awake, didn't stir. Greg and Harry Hazelton soon tumbled out of their bunks. Then something odd dawned upon them.

"Where are the rest of the fellows?" questioned Greg. "I don't see Dave, Tom or Dan."

"You should have long range vision to see them," smiled Dick. "They've been gone nearly an hour."

"Gone? Where?" Harry wanted to know.

"To the nearest house—for help."

"Help against what?" This from Holmes.

"Greg, the shack behind us had a tenant last night," Dick went on rapidly. "Mr. Fits was in the shack. At a little after five this morning I saw him as plainly as I now see you. He was standing by the nearest window of the shack, and there were sparks traveling up the chimney."

"How on earth did you see him?" demanded Harry. "Did you shove a shutter back?"

"Come with me, and I'll show you."

That caught even Hen, who made up in curiosity what he lacked in courage. Dutcher was out of his bunk in an instant, slipping on shoes and some clothing before he followed the others.

"You see," Dick was explaining, "I've been thinking of this matter ever since we heard the first 'ghost' noises. I knew the noises had to come from something. Now, while I was scared, I don't believe in such things as ghosts. Well, then, the noise must have come from some human throat. When I got up at five this morning I began to think harder than ever. Then I went and got this gimlet out of the little tool box and bored a tiny hole through the wood in this shutter. When I peeped I saw a light, surely enough, in the shack. There were sparks, too, coming up out of the chimney. Then I saw a shadow, and next I saw Mr. Fits himself at the window for a moment. Next I waked up Dave, Tom and Dan, and they dressed as quietly as they could, and took some peeps, too. Then Dave said it was so cold that perhaps the snow had a real crust on it. He went to the door and opened it. We all went out on the snow. We found the crust so hard and thick that we could stamp on it with force. Dave said that that was a good enough crust for him. So off he started, and Tom and Dan went with him. They ought to be back, with men to help, in an hour more."

"Hurrah!" glowed Greg. "Oh, I do hope that the constables get here in time to nab Mr. Fits."

"It'll be a good thing, all around, if that happens," nodded Dick. "But now—are you fellows hungry?"

Greg and Harry scurried away to wash hands and faces.

"I think you had a cheek to let three fellows go after help," grumbled Hen.

"Well, why?" asked Dick patiently.

"S'pose old Fitsey takes it into his head to come over here, on top of the crust, while there's just us four here?" shuddered Hen.

"There are only three of us here, Dutcher. You don't count," interposed Greg ironically.

"Fitsey'd eat us up alive if he guessed the truth and came over here," contended Dutcher stubbornly. "Hey, Dick! What on earth are you doing?"

"Shoving one of the shutters back," Prescott answered, going on with his task.

"Hey! Don't do that!" pleaded Hen hoarsely, running over to Dick and grabbing one of the latter's arms. "Why, this is—it's suicide, that's what it is!"

"Yes?" Dick queried calmly, shaking off Hen's hold and going on with his task.

"It certainly is," Dutcher maintained fearfully. "Why, with a shutter open, Fitsey can jump right through the window glass and be in here on top of us in a jiffy. Please close the shutter."

"Not much!" Prescott rejoined energetically, and threw back the shutter in question. "This window doesn't look out upon the shack, but it does look out the way that Dave and the others will return. I want to see the fellows when they come."

"Of course; we all do," Greg broke in. "Dick you keep your eye mainly on the landscape beyond the window. Harry and I will get breakfast."

Dutcher groaned over the risk he knew they were taking, but he felt certain that no word of his would change the plan, so he wisely held his peace after that.

But breakfast was on and eaten, and still there was no sign of returning Grammar School boys.

"Dave and his crowd must-'a' gone through the deep snow at some point where it was soft," wailed Hen. "That's just what they've done."

"Oh—dry up!" Greg retorted.

"If they ain't back here in another hour you fellows will feel the same way I do about it," Hen Dutcher predicted stubbornly.

Dick Prescott made no answer, though, truth to tell, he was beginning to worry inwardly. A mishap in the forest, on this bitterly freezing morning, would be no simple matter.

CHAPTER XVII

HEN TURNS HIS VOICE LOOSE

"I see some one coming!" called Greg, who, after breakfast, had taken up the post by the unshuttered window.

Crash! Hen Dutcher dropped the crockery plate he was drying, then plunged headlong into Dick's bunk, burrowing under the blankets.

"It's our crowd!" cried Dick joyously, as he leaped to Greg Holmes's side. "And there are two men with 'em."

"Oh, pshaw! Why didn't you say so before?" came in a half smothered voice as Dutcher thrust his head partly from under the blankets. Then he added, suddenly, in a quaking voice:

"Say, you fellows better hide—quick! If old Fitsey is in the cook shack there's bound to be some shooting."

With that Dutcher hid his head once more. But Dick, Greg and Harry paid no heed to him. They were busy getting on coats, caps and mittens. A few moments later they had the door open, and stood out on the hard crust of snow, waiting to receive the approaching party.

Dave espied them, and waved one hand without calling.

"You'd better get back in here! You'll get hurt!" warned Hen Dutcher, standing well back from the doorway.

Like a flash Dick leaped for the doorway.

"Hen, you keep quiet in there. Don't set up a yell at the very time when a little stealth is needed."

"But it's dangerous to fool with people like Fitsey!" choked Hen.

"Keep quiet! If you can't help, don't hinder. Don't be an utter pinhead, Hen."

Now that they were in sight of the cabin, Dave and his companions, and the two men with them, put on extra speed. Dick stole off to meet the approaching ones.

"Fits hasn't gotten away, has he?" hailed Dave, in a hoarse undertone.

"We haven't seen him go," Dick replied. "For all we know he's still in the shack. Officers?"

Dick indicated the two men.

"One of them is a constable," nodded Dave; "the other is a neighbor sworn in as a deputy."

"If your thief is around here, sonny," grinned the constable, "we'll soon have him where he won't trouble you. Easy, now, with the talk. We don't want to give the fellow any warning."

The constable and his deputy slipped down in front of the log cabin, followed by the boys.

"Look out! That rascal will shoot!" screamed Hen, in an agony of fear about something.

At that instant the door of the shack flew open. The two men were just in time to see Mr. Fits step out, on snowshoes. In another instant Dick & Co., behind the officers, also got a glimpse of the fellow.

"Hold on, there, neighbor," advised the constable coolly. "Just wait until we have a word with you."

Officer and deputy ran over the snowcrust. Mr. Fits, looking, or pretending to be, a bit dazed, stood as if he expected to wait for the men to come up with him. But suddenly a grin appeared on the face of the rascal.

"Fine morning and fine crust for a race," he announced, and moved away a few yards, with an easy gliding movement, on the snowshoes.

"Halt, there!" called the constable firmly, reaching back to his hip pocket.

The deputy reached for his revolver, but, in his excitement, instead of aiming or firing, he hurled the weapon at the head of Mr. Fits. The pistol went by the head of the rascal, then struck the crust and skimmed on ahead of him.

"Much obliged!" called back Fits, now moving fast.

"Don't try to pick up that weapon!" shouted the constable, running as swiftly as he could over the crust. "If you do, I'll shoot."

"I reckon you'll shoot anyway," jeered Fits, making a swoop and picking up the revolver that had been thrown at him.

Constable Dock fired promptly. But Fits wheeled, a weapon now in his own hand.

Three jets of fire leaped swiftly from the muzzle of the pistol. Three sharp explosions followed, and bullets whistled back over the snow.

Constable Dock halted, dropping to one knee, for one of the leaden pellets had gone close to his left ear. One of the bullets hit a tree just behind Prescott with a spiteful chug. Dick felt queer, but he was too much in motion to stop himself just then.

"Stop or I'll bring you down!" bellowed Constable Dock, taking careful aim. An instant later the officer fired, but at that very instant Mr. Fits skimmed off at a sharp angle with his late course, and so he escaped uninjured.

A derisive shout came back from the fugitive. He was now out of range of the officer's revolver, and knew it. The constable, too, realized the fact. He started in pursuit as rapidly as he could make it, calling to his deputy to follow.

"Going to join the chase?" called Dave to Dick.

"What's the use?" panted Prescott, halting. "Mr. Fits has a good start and can make fine speed. We could catch only the constable."

So the Grammar School boys slowed down. Constable Dock and his deputy were now almost out of sight among the trees, and no eye among the boys could see how much in the lead Mr. Fits was.

"They'll never catch him," sighed Dave.

"I'm afraid not," agreed Dick.

"And so, one of these nights, Mr. Fits will come back, ready to pay us back for our plan to turn him over to the police."

"We took care of him before, didn't we?" Prescott wanted to know.

"Yes; but Fits was alone, then, and the blizzard kept him from getting away to get help of his own choice kind. Now he can travel as much as he likes. We'll hear from him again, all right," Dave Darrin wound up.

"If we do, then we'll find a way to take care of him once more," hinted Prescott.

"Or we might vote that we've had a jolly good lot of camping, and go home," suggested Harry.

"What? Let that rascal chase us out of the woods?" flared Dick. "All who want to go home may start. I'll stay here as long as I want to, even if I have to camp alone."

"You know pretty well, Dick, that you won't have to stay in camp alone," offered Dave.

"Of course not," agreed Tom Reade. "We'll all stick. We'll hope that Fitsey won't come back. If he does, then we'll try to make him sorry that he returned."

From the doorway of the log cabin Hen Dutcher was seen to be peering forth cautiously.

"Say, you fellows," hailed Hen complainingly, "I thought

you were never coming back. I thought you had all got scared and ran away."

"Then why didn't you run away with us?" Dave called out.

"That isn't my style," proclaimed Dutcher, throwing out his chest. "I'm no baby."

"No; you're the one hero of the whole outfit," grinned Tom.

"Did they catch old Fitsey?" queried Hen.

"Thanks to you, Hen, they didn't," Dave answered.

"Me? What did I have to do with the scoundrel getting away?" demanded Dutcher, with an offended air.

"You had to turn your voice loose," Darrin informed him. "That gave Mr. Fits warning. Then you yelled out again, just as we reached the cabin. Fits had had time to get on his snowshoes, and then he started. Whew, but snowshoes seem to be as swift as skates would be on the ice."

"Huh! You needn't blame me," sniffed Hen. "I didn't have anything to do with the rascal getting away. I'd have gone after him if I had had snowshoes."

The absurdity of this was so apparent that Dick & Co. burst into a chorus of laughter.

"Huh!" sneered Hen, though his face went very red. "You fellows think you're the only winds that ever blew."

"You wrong us, Hen," declared Tom solemnly. "Not one of us would lay any claim to 'blowing' as much as you do."

One thing the boys had noted, even while carrying on their conversation, and that was that no sounds of shots had come to their ears. The chances were that Mr. Fits had gained so on his pursuers that the latter had given up the chase.

Presently appetite asserted itself, and dinner was prepared and eaten. It was after the meal that Constable Dock and his deputy came by the door.

"Any thing in there to eat, youngsters?" inquired the constable, looking in through the doorway.

"Plenty, I think. Come in, sir—you and your friend," Dick made answer.

The boys bustled about, making coffee, broiling steak and reheating the potatoes that had been left over from their own meal. This, with bread and butter, satisfied the hunger of their guests.

In the meantime the constable described how he and his friend had followed the game for some five miles or more.

"It's my opinion that the scoundrel won't come back here at all," declared the officer.

"We have been afraid that he would, by night, or later," admitted Dick Prescott.

"No!" retorted the constable with emphasis. "That rascal would figure that I would be lying in wait here for him. So he'll give the spot a wide berth. He doesn't want to be arrested."

"You'll be welcome to use the cook shack, if you want to wait there for him," volunteered Dick.

"Not a bit of use, my boy. I'd only be wasting my time. You've seen your last of that fellow around here. But now, another matter. One of your mates told me, Prescott, that you had uncovered a lot of plunder here in the cabin."

"Yes, sir; we did," Dick admitted.

"Where is it?" questioned the constable.

Dick started toward the new hiding place, then halted, turning.

"May I ask, Mr. Dock, why you want to know?"

"Because," replied the constable promptly, "as an officer of the law I want to take that plunder in charge. In turn I'll hand it over to the Gridley police."

"Oh, all right, sir."

Dick went to the hiding place, bringing forth all the plunder, including his own watch and his mother's fan.

"You'll give us a receipt for these articles, won't you, Mr. Dock?"

"Certainly, if you want one," nodded the constable. "Just place the stuff on the table, and I'll list it."

This was done, and Constable Dock wrote out a receipt in due form, which he handed to young Prescott.

"And now I'll be off and away," said the constable, rising and pulling on a heavy, short hunting coat. "I'll telephone to the Gridley police, of course. You won't see the rascal again. Rest easy on that score."

"I hope we won't see him," muttered Dave, as the boys stood outside the cabin watching the departing officers.

"If we do we'll get out of it better than Mr. Fits does, anyway," half boasted Dick.

CHAPTER XVIII

YOUNG MR. COME-BACK & CO.

"Say, you fellows—" began Hen, stepping out and joining Dick & Co.

All six turned to gaze at Dutcher. Then they looked at each other, the same thought in six minds. It was Dick who spoke:

"Hen, we came near overlooking the fact that this is your chance to get back to your friends. Get on your coat, your cap and mittens, and—"

"Whatcher talking about?" demanded Dutcher, looking almost startled.

"Hey! Mr. Dock!" bellowed Dave, using his hands as a megaphone.

The rather distant constable turned to look back.

"Please wait! There's a boy to go with you," Dave called.

"A-a-a-ll right," the answer came back.

"Hurry, Hen," Dick advised.

"But—but I don't want to go," protested Hen.

"You'd better," Dick advised him. "We housed you while it was necessary, but now there's a chance to get back to your uncle's, so you may as well go."

"I don't want—"

"Never mind about that," Dick continued firmly. "You'll be better off at your uncle's, and Constable Dock is headed that way."

"But my uncle doesn't want me," whined Hen.

"Then why should you think we can endure you, Hen, if your uncle can't?" demanded Tom Reade, with a short laugh.

"Don't keep the constable waiting, Hen," Dick pressed him. "Get your motion started."

"Oh, well, if you fellows want to be mean, I suppose I'll have to go," faltered Hen. "But I was enjoying myself here."

"You'll enjoy yourself better still with your aunt," Dick urged with a smile. "Besides, you'll have your aunt's good cooking and a real bed to sleep in. If the country highways aren't broken out yet, they will be in a day or two, and then you can get back to Gridley."

"All right, if you fellows bounce me out of camp," sighed Hen ruefully, as he began to pull on his overcoat. "But I think you're about the meanest—"

"Save the rest of it, Anvil, if you please, until we're all at home in Gridley," Dave begged him.

"Say, you stop calling me Anvil," snarled Dutcher. "I don't like that name."

"Why not?" pursued Dave. "It fits you."

"Tell that boy to hurry up, if he's going with us," bawled Mr. Dock from a distance.

"Brace, Hen," Tom advised. "There, now you're ready. Good-bye, and come again when you're grown up."

"Those fellows don't know much about good manners," thought Hen Dutcher ruefully, as he started to run over the snow crust.

"Now that Hen is gone we'll be able to stay here a day or two longer," Dave announced. "We'll have the food to do it with."

"There's one good point about Hen Dutcher, anyway," grimaced Tom Reade. "He's a good, sincere eater."

"He was eating us out of camp," Dick replied. "Now, fellows, with Hen and Fits gone, we're all by ourselves—just the crowd that we want. The snowcrust will bear, and we can move about. We ought to have a jolly time tramping about through the woods."

"Hunting!" proposed Harry. "We've got the air rifle."

"Fishing," added Tom. "We brought tackle on purpose. We must be able to find some pond hereabouts."

"But say!" Dick suddenly interjected. "Do you fellows realize that we haven't been in the old shack since Mr. Fits left it? Queer as it may seem to some of you, I believe that

Fitsey had a hiding place even in that little room. Let's go in there and see what we can root out in the way of mystery explained."

All six of the boys trooped around to the smaller structure at the rear of their camp. The door was still partly open. Dick, in advance, pushed his way inside.

"Well of all the boobies, what do you think of us?" demanded young Prescott, in deep disgust.

"We wouldn't take any blue ribbons at a brains' show—that's certain," affirmed Tom Reade.

The cook shack went up to a pitched roof. Up under the roof some brackets had been made fast to the rafters. These brackets held a quantity of rough boards that looked as though they had been stored up there, years ago, to season indoors. Now, a rope hung down from this artificial garret.

"Let's see what we can find up there," suggested Dick. Taking hold of the rope, after shedding his overcoat, Prescott ascended, hand over hand.

"This is where Fitsey stayed daytimes," Dick called down. "And it's not a bad place, either. Here are two fur robes."

Dick tumbled them down below, followed by four pairs of warm blankets.

"It's all stolen stuff, I'll wager," Tom called.

"Likely enough," agreed Dick.

"See if you can find a lot of gold and gems up there," proposed Greg Holmes.

"Nothing in that line. But stand below, two of you, and catch."

Dick began to toss down canned goods, sealed paper cartons of crackers, canned fruits and the like.

"And to think that Fitsey took some of our poor food, when he had a grocery store like that up aloft!" complained Harry Hazelton.

"Well, he didn't want us to suspect what he had hidden away around the premises," Dick answered.

"Anything more up there?" called Dave.

"Nothing but one Grammar School boy," Dick announced, showing himself at the edge of the simple loft. "I'm coming down. Each of you climb up here, in turn, and see what a bully hiding place our old college chum had."

One after another the boys inspected the place. It was small, but every inch had been made to count by the late occupant.

"Fitsey pulled the rope up after him, and stayed here sleeping mostly in the daytime," Tom called down, when aloft. "Say, fellows, after this, when we're on the trail of a mystery, we want to look on the other side of anything as big as a lumber pile."

Blankets, fur robes and food were transferred to the log cabin.

"But just how much better are we than thieves?" Greg suddenly asked. "We've just been taking things that didn't belong to us."

For a moment or two that was a poser, for every member of Dick & Co. tried, always, to be as open and honest as the day itself.

"Oh, well," grunted Dick at last, "we haven't been robbing Mr. Fits, for a man of his habits never has anything of his own. All that he has he steals from some one else."

"Then ought we not to try to find owners for the food we've brought in from the shack?" queried Dave.

"Yes; if we can," agreed Dick. "But I doubt if the former rightful owners of this food stuff would know their own goods. It's just such stuff as one might find in anyone of a thousand grocery stores. We couldn't identify any of these cans, ourselves, if we found it in any one else's house. You see, these labels are all of common brands of tinned foods. On the whole, fellows, I believe we have a clear right to eat this food if we happen to need it while we're in the woods. It isn't like stuff that a former owner could remember and identify."

The more they talked it over, the clearer this view became to the Grammar School boys.

"We've time for a couple of hours of hunting, now, if any of you care to go," Dick suggested. "We'll have daylight that long. But it won't do, with any chance of Mr. Fits being about, for all of us to go at once. We must leave at least two of the fellows, and they must close the shutters and keep the bar on the door. The two fellows who stay behind can also begin to get things ready against the supper hour. I'll be one of the two to stay. Who'll be the other."

"No, you won't, Dick Prescott," retorted Greg. "You've been taking first tricks at all the hard work. You've worked like a horse in this camp. To-day you'll take the first trick at having some of the fun. I'll be one of the two to stay in camp."

Dan also volunteered. Thereupon the other four, Harry carrying the air rifle, started off into the woods, jogging along over the solid crust. Though the air was keenly cold, to the boys it was all delightful. They were warmly clad, even their feet being protected by heavy overshoes. With caps drawn down over their ears, and warm mittens on their hands, why should they mind if the mercury stood somewhat below zero?

Three of them were out on a trip of exploration. Hazelton, however, was the young Nimrod. He wanted to bag a rabbit! Yet, seeing no game, Harry finally persuaded Tom Reade to carry the rifle.

Then at last, all unexpectedly, Hazelton caught sight of a rabbit. The little animal had hopped briskly over the snow, coming within sight of the Grammar School boys. Ears pointing straight up, the rabbit sat on its haunches, curiously gazing at these humans.

"Tom! Psst! ps-st! Halt!" called Harry hoarsely over the snow.

"Hey?" answered Reade, and all four came to a halt.

"There's a rabbit," called Harry softly, pointing.

"Bless me, so there is," agreed Tom.

"Well, why don't you shoot it? What are you carrying that air rifle for?"

"To oblige you, I guess," responded Tom, not making any

motion to raise the rifle. "If you want to shoot the rabbit, come here and get the rifle."

"If I move it will scare him away," protested Hazelton. "Quick! Get him before he goes off on a run!"

Sighting, Tom raised the rifle, glancing through the sights at the little white furred thing.

"Confound him! He looks too cute for anything," muttered Tom. "I haven't the heart—"

Abruptly Reade lowered the air rifle.

"See here, Harry, if your mouth is watering for rabbit stew you come here and get the gun, and do the shooting yourself. I'd feel like a criminal, taking the life of that cute, innocent little thing!"

"Huh!" growled Harry.

"Come here and get the rifle, if you want to shoot," insisted Tom.

Harry looked about as queer as he felt, for a moment. Then, picking up a piece of branch that had blown from a tree, Hazelton shied it at the rabbit, which promptly scampered away.

"That's much the better way to go hunting," nodded Dick approvingly.

After that no more was said about hunting. Tom continued to carry the air rifle, though plainly the weapon was all for show.

By and by the Grammar School boys came across a pond, an eighth of a mile wide, with a brook emptying into it.

"It will be worth while bringing the tackle to this place tomorrow, and trying for fish," proposed Dick.

"And then, if you get one, you'll get a tender hearted streak and put it right back in the water," grumbled Harry.

"Perhaps," Dick laughed. "But say, fellows, the sun is setting, and we're a good way from camp. Hadn't we better turn back?"

"My empty stomach says 'yes,'" nodded Darrin. So the youngsters trudged back over their course. It was dark before they got near the log cabin.

"Ha, ha, ha!" came a croaking laugh from inside the cabin as Dick and his chums neared the door. "That's a good one."

"Hen Dutcher's voice!" muttered Dave. "How on earth did that fellow get back here?"

Dick reached for the latch-string, opening the door. Then these four Grammar School boys received a big surprise.

Hen Dutcher was there, but so were Fred Ripley, Bert Dodge and a half dozen other young fellows, all of them older and larger than the members of Dick & Co. To make the intrusion still more impudent, Ripley's crowd were all at table, eating the best that the cabin afforded.

CHAPTER XIX

NOT A LOVE FEAST

At the same instant that Dick and his friends, all utterly astounded, peered into the cabin from the doorway, Fred Ripley felt the draught and looked around.

"Hullo!" shouted Fred gleefully. "Here are the other babies!"

"What are you fellows trying to do here?" demanded Dick sternly, as he strode into the cabin.

"Minding our business, booby!" leered Fred.

"You've no right here. Get out!" Dick ordered.

All of the intruding feasters were now regarding Prescott mockingly. But perhaps Hen Dutcher, who was seated on the furthest side of the table from the door, was most pleased of all.

"Now, you want to shut your mouth, Dick Prescott, and keep it shut," advised Hen. "You're not running this show, and you'll find it out mighty soon if you don't keep your tongue behind your teeth."

"My, how brave you've grown, Hen!" remarked Dick scornfully. "You were taken in and looked after, and now you've brought this gang of hoodlums down on us."

"Be careful there, small boy!" warned Fred Ripley, flushing.

"As for you, Ripley," Dick went on, "wouldn't your father be proud to find you with a crowd like this, and stealing food that belongs to other people?"

"See here, you little rat," snarled Fred inelegantly, as he leaped up, kicking his chair over and striding toward the Prescott group, "you want to keep your tongue under control, or you're going to be sorry that you didn't."

"Let's take the kid down to the spring, break the ice and give his head a soaking in the spring water," proposed Bert Dodge, rising, too, and coming forward.

"Hurrah!" cheered Hen. "That's the stuff. Not a bit too good, either, for a chump like Dick Prescott!"

But Dick wouldn't pay any heed to this renegade Grammar School boy who had gone back on his own mates.

"And where are the two friends we left here?" demanded Dick, undismayed by the advance of Fred Ripley and Bert Dodge. Tom and Dave drew a little closer to their chum, while Harry Hazelton flanked Dave.

"What do we know about your friends?" sneered Ripley. "What do we know about any of your cheap crowd?"

"And what do you imagine we care about them, either?" demanded Dodge.

"Are you fellows going to get out of here?" Dick demanded.

"When we get good and ready," retorted Fred, grinning. "That may be to-morrow or the next day."

"I suppose," Dick went on angrily, "you think you have a perfect right to stay here and to go on stealing our food?"

"You call me a thief, do you?" flared Fred.

"Do you consider yourself any better?" Dick asked. He was at white heat, fighting mad, and cared little what he said to these rowdyish intruders.

"Grab 'em, fellows!" ordered Fred, making a leap at Dick, while the other intruders rose from their places at table.

But Dick's right fist landed on Ripley's face, leaving a big, red mark there, while Dave's ready foot tripped the bully, sending him to the floor. Ripley was on his feet again in a twinkling.

"Get back, Ripley!" ordered Dick, making a dash at him. "See here, you rowdy, I'm smaller than you are, but I'm willing to go outdoors with you and see if I can't teach you some manners."

"And I'll take pleasure in introducing myself to Bert Dodge at the same time," announced Darrin, his eyes flashing.

"I'll do my best with any other tough who'll oblige me," added Tom Reade.

"Bullies, toughs, rowdies, are we?" raged Fred Ripley, on his guard, though just prudent enough to keep out of reach of Dick's fists. There was a look in Prescott's eyes that the lawyer's self-willed son didn't wholly like.

"You fellows know just what you are," Dick went on bitterly. "There is no use in our calling you names. You can supply the names yourselves. And, if you're afraid to fight us, man to man, then you know well enough what else you are! Now, what has become of Greg Holmes and Dan Dalzell?"

"Oh, very likely they're still running as fast as they can go toward Gridley," jeered Fred.

"That's a lie, and no one knows it better than you!" flashed Dick. "Greg and Dan are not of the running kind."

"Oh, I'm a liar, also, am I?" choked Ripley.

"You know yourself better than any one else can," was Prescott's taunting answer.

"Come on, fellows!" urged Fred. "Rush 'em!"

There was a prompt rush. Dick and his friends did not flinch, but met the attack squarely. Hen Dutcher was the only boy present who did not display much eagerness to get at too close quarters in the fray.

"Give it to 'em!" cheered Dutcher, hopping about at a safe distance while the scuffle went on. "They need plenty! Give Dick Prescott and Darrin each an extra one for me."

The odds against more numerous and larger boys were so heavy that it was not long ere Dick, Dave, Tom and Harry were borne down to the dirt floor. Nor were they handled generously. All four received many an unfair blow. Fred's temper was up, for Dick had struck him on the nose, bringing blood.

"Now we'll give 'em the rope treatment," laughed Ripley, hoarsely, when Dick and his chums had all been downed and were being held.

First a noose was slipped over Dick's wrists, and made fast. Dave was the next so favored. Tom and Harry rapidly shared that fate.

"Now lead these cattle to the stable!" roared Fred, gripping Dick by the collar and yanking him to his feet.

The battle being lost, Dick and the others could do no more than submit to being pushed outside the cabin, Hen Dutcher following and making faces at all of the captives.

Around to the cook shack the four Grammar School boys were led. The door was flung open, and in they were thrust.

There on the floor, bound hand and foot and gagged, lay Greg and Dan. These two members of Dick & Co. had been overpowered and placed here, but only one look at their faces was needed to show that both still had their fighting blood up.

"Now, don't let us hear anything from you boobies," commanded Fred Ripley, "or I'll send a committee out here to attend to you in mighty short order!"

Then the door of the cook shack was closed on Dick & Co.

"Well, of all the downright mean tricks!" grumbled Tom Reade.

"That's too complimentary a name for such human truck!" cried Dave Darrin angrily. "Their first scheme, to come down here in the night and try to scare us, wasn't so fearfully mean, but this is assault and robbery."

"Never mind about it, now," Dick answered. "Our wrath will keep—no doubt about that. But our first task is to get our hands free, if we can. And Greg and Dan must feel pretty tired of being gagged as well as tied."

A snort, the only noise he could make, was Greg Holmes's answer.

"How are we going to get ourselves free?" Tom demanded: "I've been trying to wriggle my hands out, but I'll admit that I can't do it."

"Get over here in front of me," urged Dick, "and I'll show you just how I can free you. Fred Ripley, like other blunderers, is likely to overlook a few things."

It was not cold in the cook shack, for there was still some fire going in the stove. The embers also threw a slight amount of illumination into the room.

Dick dropped to his knees behind Tom Reade, and, reaching for the cords that bound Tom's wrists behind his back, began to gnaw.

"Well, by hokey!" gasped Tom. "I never had head enough to think of that."

"If we were gagged like Greg and Dan, we couldn't do the trick," Dave rejoined. "Come here, Harry; get in front of me and I'll gnaw your wrists free."

Dick paused long enough in his work to say:

"No need, Dave. When Tom is once free he can use his knife

and have us all turned loose in a jiffy."

Prescott possessed strong, fine teeth. He gnawed away at the cords to such good advantage that Reade soon had the use of his hands.

"Now, I'll do as much for you, Dick," Tom proposed, reaching for his pocket knife.

Within a very short time all six were free, and Greg and Dan, their mouths free of the gags, told indignantly how they had been engaged in preparing supper when the door opened and Ripley and his crowd burst in.

"And now I suppose the rowdies are eating up the supper," finished Greg vengefully.

"I guess they've got it about finished by now," Prescott added grimly. "But we six are free. If we're any good we'll get our cabin back and make it our castle against all comers."

"Good!" cried Dave, a fiery flash in his eyes. "But how?"

"That's what we've got to figure out," Dick replied thoughtfully. "But we'll do it."

CHAPTER XX

THE COOK SHACK DISASTER

"First of all," Dick continued, "it's going to be chilly, soon, in this shack. Put on some fuel, Harry, won't you?"

Hazelton complied with the request. By a common instinct all of the Grammar School boys gathered closely around the stove, extending their hands and warming themselves.

"The battle can't be ours a bit too soon," observed Tom Reade dryly. "We've simply got to eat soon. Too bad we carted all of Mr. Fits's larder into the cabin this afternoon."

"But what are we going to do about retaking our cabin," pressed that budding young war horse, Darrin.

"I'm thinking fast over every plan that comes to me," Dick answered thoughtfully. "If any of you other fellows think of one first don't be backward with it. I'll promise not to be jealous."

"Hang that Dutcher hound, anyway!" growled Tom Reade angrily. "I can't get over his mean, dirty work."

"The best way is not to mention the fellow," Dick answered

coldly. "He's not worth it."

"Oh, he isn't, eh?" muttered a boy who had just stolen softly to the outside of the shack door and now stood there listening. That eavesdropper was Hen Dutcher, who had slipped out of the cabin to see how life fared with the boys whom he didn't like.

Then Hen, still eavesdropping, listened to enough more to make sure that Dick & Co. were all of them free of their bonds, and that these enterprising Grammar School boys were actually discussing plans to rout the enemy from the log cabin.

"Oh, I'll have to hustle back and tell this to Ripley's crew," chuckled Hen gleefully. "It'll amuse 'em."

"What's that?" demanded Ripley, when the informer returned to the cabin with his news. "Prescott and his collection of babies are going to make trouble for us, are they? Can't they stand a good joke like men? Come along, fellows, and we'll teach 'em a little more about being real men."

"We'd better take something in our hands, then," proposed Dodge firmly. "Those little fellows are regular spitfires. They may have something ready to throw at us when we break into the shack."

"Oh, take axes, then, if you are afraid of the little kids," retorted Fred scornfully. "My hands are enough for me."

Four or five of the rowdyish crowd picked up sticks that they had carried through the forest that afternoon. Thus prepared, they went out of the log cabin on tip-toe, making their way stealthily to the door of the shack.

"Say, fellows," Harry was at that moment proposing to his friends inside, "hadn't we better drop the bar across the door? We can't tell when we may receive an unexpected visit from—"

"How will now do?" roared Fred Ripley, throwing the shack door open before Greg could drop the bar in place. "So you young smarties managed to free yourselves, did you? And you thought you'd find a way to put a trick over on us? You'll have to take to getting up earlier in the day, if you expect to get the better of any crowd that I'm leading."

Ripley's crew were now all of them in the shack, crowding the little place.

"What is it that you're scheming to do, anyway?" leered Fred, enjoying the looks of dismay on the faces of Dick & Co. "See here, don't you little boys think that it's about time for you all to line up and start a footrace out of these woods?"

"No; we don't," Dick retorted defiantly. "We think it's high time, though, for your crowd to start just such a race."

"Hold your tongue, freshie!" ordered Fred roughly.

"Not for you!" Dick snapped, his temper going up as the mercury climbs on a hot day.

"Then I'll make you!" offered young Ripley, making a spring at Dick.

But Dick & Co. were now all together, standing in a firm fighting line. Fred received punches from the fists belonging to three different school boys, and fell back, red and panting.

"Sail in, everybody!" ordered Fred. "These simpletons haven't sense enough to stand a good joke on themselves."

It was an unmanly thing to do. Some of the boys in Ripley's crowd had no idea of going further than having rather rough "fun." However, the shack, in an instant, was the scene of a lively mix-up. In the midst of the excitement Bert Dodge drove Harry Hazelton against the stovepipe. It came down, showering soot all over Fred's face and down his neck. In the excitement that followed, and during the rush of some of the boys to get out of the flying cloud of soot, the stove itself was overturned. Red embers flew about in every direction. The door being open, the wind helped to set the cabin ablaze.

"Now you've done it!" panted Dick, holding up one hand and trying to put a stop to the trouble. "Quit fighting and help put the fire out."

"You youngsters put it out yourselves, then," Fred retorted. "It was all your fault that it started."

An indignant denial came to Dick's lips, but he forced it back. This shack was another's property, and personal differences must be kept in the background until the blaze had been extinguished.

"Let me past you," demanded Dick indignantly, but Bert Dodge barred the doorway until the mounting flames scared Ripley, who turned and yelled to Dodge to let the boys out. Dick & Co. raced to the log cabin, where they caught up the water buckets, a dishpan and other utensils that would hold water. Dick also snatched up a hatchet, for he knew that the spring would be frozen over.

Fast as they worked at the spring, the shack was well ablaze by the time that the Grammar School boys returned with the first water.

"Why don't you fellows brace up and do something, Ripley?" Dick queried, as he ran up with water.

"What is there for us to do?" Fred demanded rather soberly.

"Find something to do. Show yourself a man."

"Now, don't you turn impudent again," Ripley warned young Prescott angrily. "It was that sort of thing that started the first trouble."

"You'd better find something to do, for your father has charge of this property," Dick shot back over his shoulder, as he ran toward the spring.

"Look!" called Dave, as Dick & Co. started once more for the spring. "It's too late. This little bit of water won't do anything for the shack. See the sparks fly! They'll fall on the roof of the cabin, and that will go, too."

The blaze was now fast reaching the roof of the shack. Blazing little flakes of fire were soaring up toward the sky.

"We can't save the shack. We can't get water fast enough!" Prescott called. "We must try to wet down the roof of the cabin, to keep it from getting afire."

Fred Ripley and Bert Dodge now appeared to be thoroughly frightened. Without waiting to be asked, they came forward to help boost Dick and Dave up to the roof of the log cabin. As fast as the water came Dick or Dave dashed it over the side of the cabin roof that was more exposed to sparks from the shack, every particle of snow having been blown off the roof by the furious wind that had prevailed.

"Look!" called Tom. "The wind is coming up—it's carrying the sparks away from the cabin."

"No need to bring more water, then," sang out Fred Ripley, in a voice of intense relief. "It's all right if the sparks aren't blowing toward the cabin."

"Keep bringing water," disputed Dick, "until the shack is completely burned down. We can't take any chances."

But at last even Dick Prescott was satisfied with the quantity of water that had been poured over the cabin's roof. Before the new breeze the sparks were steadily being carried the other way.

"We'll stop, now," Dick announced. "We can start again at any time that the wind changes to this quarter."

"What are you going to tell your father about this, Ripley?" Dave Darrin asked presently.

"Nothing," replied Fred, with a start.

"Is that all you ever tell him about your misdeeds?" inquired Tom dryly.

"This isn't my misdeed," Fred snapped. "You fellows started all the trouble."

"I suppose we even invited your crowd to come over here this afternoon and steal our food?" Dave continued.

"Now, you youngsters will get trouble started all over again, if you don't look out," Fred threatened the Grammar School boys.

"You'd better leave us alone," suggested Dick, "and make up your mind about what you're going to tell your father when he hears about this."

"Who's going to tell him?" snarled young Ripley.

"I don't know."

"Are you, Dick Prescott?" insisted Fred.

"Not unless I have to."

"Don't you dare go to spreading this yarn around Gridley!"

"I won't promise," Dick made answer. "I don't want to carry tales if I can help it, but we're bound to report to your father that the cook shack was burned down while we were here."

"You can tell my father that it was your own carelessness, and let it go at that," suggested Ripley.

"Humph! I like the cool nerve of your idea," Dick jeered.

"That's what you'll tell my father, if you know what's good for you," Fred went on. "That's all I've got to say, but you'll be sorry if you don't take my advice."

Though the temperature was some degrees below zero in the forest that evening, none of the boys near the log cabin felt at all cold. The shack, whose roof soon fell in, still burned briskly enough to keep all hands warm.

"Watch your chance to dart into the cabin when you see me start. Move fast when the time comes. Tell Tom and Harry when you get a chance, but don't let the Ripley crowd suspect."

Dick then found chance to pass the message to Greg and Dan.

Five minutes later Dick sauntered back to the corner of the cabin at the front side. Dave approached from another direction. Tom and the others caught the meaning of the move. Then, all of a sudden, there was a scampering of feet.

"Look out!" yelled telltale Hen. "That crowd is up to something!"

"I know what they're up to!" shouted Fred. "Follow me!"

The older boys charged the cabin door, but they reached it just as Greg was dropping the bar into place.

"Get in through the windows—quick!" shouted Ripley. He himself made a dash for one of the windows. Click! went a shutter before his face, and the locking-pin was dropped in. In a trice all the shutters were in place.

Dick & Co. were in their castle!

"You fellows open that door!" stormed Fred Ripley.

"Come inside and make us!" mocked Dick.

"Open that door," summoned Fred, "or we'll get a log and use it for a battering ram. We can get the door down that way!"

Dick felt a throb of dismay. It would be possible to get the door down by the aid of a battering ram, if the boys outside could find a sufficiently large log and had the strength to use it.

CHAPTER XXI

ON THE TRAIL BACKWARD

"You'd better listen to me, Fred Ripley," called Dick, through the barred door.

"Yah! You better do the listening!" snarled Ripley. "Open that door, or trouble is going to start inside of sixty seconds."

"What I want to say," Dick went on, rather calmly now, since he felt that he was nearly master of the situation, "is that, if you break the door down, or start anything else that is mean, we shall have to tell your father all about it. We were given charge of this property, and we've got to account for it. You're a lawyer's son; perhaps you know what kind of trouble your conduct here to-night will get you into."

"Telltale!" taunted Fred.

Dick made no answer, deeming silence the wiser course.

"Sneak!" added Ripley.

Dick held up his hand as a signal to his chums to preserve silence. Outside the other boys heard no noise save that made by Tom Reade when he began to feed the fire, for the interior of the cabin was growing a trifle chilly.

"Now, don't say a word to them, no matter what those fellows yell at us," Dick whispered, circulating among his chums. "Don't even let them hear us talking among ourselves. If everything is still in here, and they can't get any answer from us, that may set them to guessing. If we get them to guessing they'll be uneasy next."

So silence reigned within the cabin. There was no response from Dick & Co., even when the larger boys outside kicked and pounded on the door and shouted abusive taunts.

Every now and then one of Fred's crowd would slip around by the shack and warm himself before the still glowing embers.

"We might as well cut it, and get out of this," Fred whispered at last to his companions, after he had summoned them by signs to join him before the blaze that was left at the site of the shack. "Those youngsters won't let us into their house, and we'll freeze to death around here as soon as yonder bonfire is out. We'll get back to your uncle's Hen. Bert and I have been paying him board money for the crowd, and he'll be glad enough to see us back. But let's go without making any noise, and then the youngsters in the cabin will wonder—just simply wonder—whether we've left or are still around. The result will be that they won't dare to show their noses outdoors."

So General Fred marched his forces away by stealth. Had he been able to look into the cabin, though, before departing, he would have felt chagrined.

For Messrs. Dick & Co. were far from feeling uncomfortable. They had suddenly discovered, all over again, that they were hungry. The hour being late, they had put together a light repast, and were now enjoying it. Then, not having heard anything of the enemy for an hour, Dick decided upon opening the door to take a peep outside. His five chums, however, stood at his back, while Greg Holmes held the bar, ready to drop it into place instantly at need.

As Dick looked out he saw all clear before the cabin. He stole down to the corner of the log structure, gazing at what was left of the shack blaze. There was but little of that.

Then Prescott ran around the cabin.

"Nobody in sight," he reported. "The rowdy crowd has gone home—or probably up to Hen's uncle's house. We won't see 'em again to-night."

"Let's go to bed, then," proposed Tom. "If they come back they can't get in without making a noise that will wake us."

"Bed will be a first rate idea," nodded Dick, "as soon as we have got in some wood and water."

This took barely ten minutes. The same space of time was devoted to building up the fire for the night. Then, well tired, despite all their excitement, all the members of Dick & Co. were soon sound asleep.

It was eight in the morning when the first one of them awoke.

"Well, we got through the night without having any more of either Ripley or Fits," remarked Tom, as he dressed.

"Which is worse?" inquired Dave.

"Mr. Fits, by all means," Dick replied. "We can come very close to thrashing Fred Ripley and his crew. And they can be scared away, too. But Mr. Fits is downright dangerous."

"If all outsiders, intruders and enemies will only keep away from here we can have a splendid time after this," sighed Tom.

"We're going to have a good time, anyway," Dick declared stoutly. "So far, those who have tried to annoy us have succeeded only in furnishing some excitement for us. Although we've been snowbound most of the time here we've had anything but a dull time."

"Is it safe for us all to leave camp at one time?" inquired Greg.

"If you're asking me," Dick replied, "I don't believe it is. We can't be sure that Fits, or Fred Ripley's crowd, won't swoop down here at any moment. It is just the doubt that will make us feel unwise in leaving the camp without any one to guard it. As far as Ripley is concerned, I don't believe he's going to show up here again. The burning of the cook shack, accidental though it was, has probably been enough to frighten Fred Ripley so that he and his crowd will soon start for Gridley, if they haven't headed in that direction already."

"Then suppose you and I stay here this morning," proposed Dave Darrin, "and let the other fellows get out for this morning?"

"All right," agreed Dick.

"And you'd better keep the shutters over all but one window," suggested Tom. "You can close and fasten that one quickly, at need. And, when you're inside the cabin, have the bar on the door and don't open, even to us, unless you recognize our voices."

"Why, we'll feel as if we were living in a fort, at that rate," Dick laughed.

"One has to, in the face of an enemy," Greg asserted. "But you can call it a blockhouse, instead of a fort, Dick, and the logs will look more in keeping."

Before four of the Grammar School boys departed on a forenoon tramp all hands turned to and laid in a goodly supply of firewood and water.

In the afternoon Dick and Dave headed a party of young explorers, leaving Tom and Greg on guard at the cabin.

The day after, morning and afternoon, the Grammar School boys fished through the ice on the pond, catching enough pickerel and trout to last famished boys for two meals.

During these two days neither Mr. Fits nor the Ripley crew made an appearance. Still, the camp was not left unguarded. A few more days of rare life and sport followed. Then there came a day when, an hour after sun up, the crust proved too weak to support the Grammar School boys.

"We've a thaw coming," hinted Dave.

"Or else a storm," added Prescott.

"Whatever is coming will be all right," announced Tom, "if it isn't another big blizzard. A second blizzard, and we'll be snowbound here for the rest of the winter!"

The softness of the snow kept the Grammar School boys at

the camp that day. Their stock of books came in handy now. By four o'clock that afternoon it began to rain. Soon it poured, and the downfall kept coming all night long. It was still raining heavily when the new day came. That warm rainstorm lasted until nearly evening of the second day. With every hour of continued rain some of the snow vanished.

"We're going to lose the last bit of the good white stuff," predicted Tom gloomily.

When the rain ceased at last the prophecy was verified. Throughout the forest the recent "big snow" was visible only in small patches here and there.

"The best part of our good time is gone," grumbled Dan.

"Have you fellows been watching the state of provisions lately, I wonder?" asked Dick.

"What about 'em?" demanded Harry.

"Well, just look over the stock."

"We've enough for two days yet, haven't we?"

"I don't believe what we have will last us through to-morrow," Dick went on. "Let's appoint ourselves a committee to take account of stock."

"We made a big mistake when we were figuring on what we'd need," grumbled Dan.

"No," replied Dick, with a shake of his head. "What we didn't allow for, in the first place, was boarding a huge eater like Hen Dutcher for a while. Nor did we plan to have Ripley's crowd here in our absence, helping themselves and wasting almost as much as they used."

"Whew!" grunted Tom disconsolately. "We've soon got to be hitting the home trail, haven't we?"

"Or else go to bed to-morrow night on a small allowance of food," nodded Dick, "and prepared to do without food the day after that."

There was much discussion that night. Tom was for "sticking it out," doing the best possible on a diet of fish that might be caught in the pond. But wiser counsel prevailed. Early next morning Dick and Dave started out over the bare ground on their way to the nearest house that had a telephone. It proved to be Constable Dock's house, though the officer himself was away. Calling up Miller's grocery store, Mr. Miller's son, Joe, was engaged to come out to camp at once with a wagon.

It was late in the afternoon, however, when Joe arrived. It took another hour for the boys to get their outfit packed on to the wagon. Then they seated themselves on top of the load and Joe clucked to the horses.

"So you boys ran across the fit thrower out in the woods, and he gave you plenty of excitement?" queried Joe, after the start homeward had been made.

"Yes," nodded Dick, "and we were afraid he'd show up again before we got through in the woods."

"Why?" asked Joe, bringing the whip down lazily on the flanks of the horses.

"Because," Dick answered, "we found his loot, and he knew we had found it. We feared that he'd make another big effort to get back the stuff, which was valuable."

H. Irving Hancock

"But the police have the stuff," Joe went on.

"How do you know that?"

"Why, Ripley's crowd knew it when they got back to Gridley, and the newspapers got the fact from the Gridley police."

"If Mr. Fits read the Gridley papers," remarked Prescott, thoughtfully, "then of course he knew he couldn't recover any of his plunder by paying us a visit. That, I guess, was the only reason why he didn't pay the cabin another visit."

"That, and the other fact, perhaps," Joe went on, "that the Gridley papers hinted that the cabin was being shadowed by the police."

"But it wasn't."

"No matter; if your fit throwing gentleman thought he was going to take any chances of running into police out in these woods, then he wasn't going to slip his neck into a noose."

"I'm glad he kept away," muttered Tom Reade.

"Unless we could have had the pleasure of jumping on the rascal and getting the glory of capturing him," flashed Dave Darrin.

"I feel a bit blue over leaving the good old cabin," complained Greg Holmes.

"So would I," returned Dick, "if it weren't for the fact that Lawyer Ripley told us we could use the place whenever we choose. That means that we can go camping there again."

"Maybe Lawyer Ripley will take back what he said when he hears about the cook shack being burned to the ground," suggested Harry solemnly.

"But we didn't burn it down, anyway," retorted Dick.

"Who did, then?" asked Joe curiously.

None of Dick & Co., however, offered an answer.

After glancing at the boys in turn, Joe decided to hold his peace on that topic.

It was well after dark when the outfit arrived in Gridley. Joe drove to Dick's first, with that youngster's belongings. The other boys jumped from the "rig" and scurried homeward for supper.

"Young man," was Mr. Prescott's greeting of his son, "from all I hear, you boys went in for a bigger list of adventure than you outlined to us before starting away."

"It wasn't on account of any wishes of ours, Dad," laughed Dick. "We fairly had the extra excitement thrust on us."

"I hope you've had a good time, my son, and supper is ready for you," remarked Mrs. Prescott practically.

"Run upstairs with your mother and have your meal," directed the elder Prescott. "I'll watch the store while your mother is thrilling over the doings of the week."

"Mother," was one of Dick's first questions upstairs, "did Dan's homing pigeon get back with our message?"

"Oh, yes."

"Then all you parents were easy about our safety."

"Quite. But I can't tell you how worried I was when I heard of your adventures with that terrible thief."

"He didn't bother us much, mother. We were small boys, but there were too many of us."

"But suppose he had shot one of you?"

"He didn't have any firearms, mother, until one of the officers made the mistake of throwing a pistol at him."

Then Dick had to go over all the adventures of the snowbound days.

"As soon as I clear up here," said Mrs. Prescott, "I'm going down into the store and tell your father some of the exciting things you've been telling me. And I know, Richard, that you're anxious to get out on the street and see some of your schoolmates. So run along."

Dick had not been out five minutes before he encountered Dave Darrin.

"Let's go up Main Street and see if we can't run into Tom and some of the other fellows," proposed Dave.

"Good enough," Dick nodded. But they went a good many blocks without encountering any of their own crowd.

"Wait; I want to step into this doorway and tie my shoe," said Dave. Dick took a few steps ahead. Just at the corner he encountered a man slinking around into Main Street.

"You here?" gasped Dick, then instantly he went down under

a blow on his chest.

"Dave!" gasped Prescott, rather badly winded.

"What?" demanded Darrin, racing up.

"Mr. Fits knocked me down and bolted around that corner," flashed Dick Prescott.

CHAPTER XXII

HEN DUTCHER IS MODEST

For an instant Dave hesitated, reluctant to leave a comrade injured.

"Get after him!" ordered young Prescott, rising somewhat slowly. "Don't let the fellow get out of sight."

At that direct command Dave Darrin darted around the corner, going fast down the side street. A moment later Dick hove into sight, though some distance to the rear of his now more agile chum.

As he ran Darrin felt like rubbing his eyes. By the aid of the street lamps he could see fairly well down to the next corner. The fugitive hadn't had time to cover all that distance in the few moments that he had been out of view.

"Dave!" called Dick, though his voice at first wasn't very loud. Darrin didn't hear, though a moment later he halted, glancing about him and back at his chum. Prescott was beckoning.

"He has darted in somewhere on this block," muttered Dick, as his chum reached him.

"Yes," Dave agreed; "but where?"

"That's too much for us to guess."

"What are we going to do about it?"

"I don't know," Dick confessed disappointedly. "I hate to see Mr. Fits slip away from us like this, though."

"Well, he has done it, anyway," Dave declared. "I'm afraid there isn't much that we can do now."

"We can go down to the next corner, and back on the other side," Dick Prescott proposed. "Look back frequently, Dave, and, if you see Mr. Fits dart out of any house or doorway, then yell to me, and we'll both turn and race after the fellow."

"A nice sprinter you'll make, after that knock down blow on the chest," remarked Darrin dryly.

"Oh, I'm getting a little more wind back every minute," Dick declared cheerily. "I could run, now, if I had to, and in two minutes from now I'll be able to do a whole lot better. Come along. You do the turning to look backward, and I'll use my eyes in front of us."

In this fashion they explored the entire block on both sides. Their slow, thorough search at last brought them back to Main Street, much puzzled and not a little discouraged.

"What now?" inquired Dave.

"We've done all we can," Dick replied, "except find a policeman and tell him that we've seen Fits back in town."

"It's strange that he should come back to Gridley," murmured

Darrin. "You'd think that the fellow would be anxious to give the town a wide berth."

"Undoubtedly he has his reasons. But—Dave, there's a policeman. Let's hurry and tell him."

In another moment the two Grammar School boys were engaged in reciting what had happened to a uniformed member of the night police force of Gridley.

"There's no time to be lost," declared the policeman. "For a matter as important as this I'll leave my beat and notify the station house."

"Can we give you any further help?" Dick asked.

"Not a bit, my lad, thank you, unless you see Fitsey again."

As soon as the policeman had gone, Darrin asked rather seriously:

"Dick, are you sure that it really was Fits, and no mistake?"

"Of course I am. Why?"

"Oh, nothing, only it seems so strange to me that the fellow should really venture back into the one town where the police are really anxious to land him."

"It was Mr. Fits that I saw," Prescott insisted. "Besides, no one else would want to knock me down."

"That's so," Dave admitted. "Well, I hope that the police find the rascal."

"It's a lot more likely that we, or some of our fellows, will do the finding," laughed Prescott. "We've done all the finding so far."

At this moment a hand smote Dick heavily between the shoulders, while Tom Reade's laughing voice demanded:

"Fellows, how does home cooking seem again? Isn't it great?"

Harry Hazelton was with Tom.

"We've almost forgotten how good the home cooking is," Dick answered. "We've just had something else to think about."

Then the story of the latest meeting with Mr. Fits was told.

"Jupiter!" breathed Tom excitedly. "Say, I wish we could run that fellow down. I'm just aching to pay him back for the night of ghost scare that he gave us out in the forest!"

"I'd like well enough to see him caught," Dick agreed. "But I can't say that I want to do it myself."

"Why not?" challenged Tom.

"Well, he's a powerful big brute, and I doubt if we four could handle Mr. Fits."

"Huh!" retorted Tom. "I'd like to try it, anyway. And, if we had the chance, and missed, four of us could make noise enough to bring a few men to our aid."

"That part would be all right," Dick agreed. "If we see the rascal again it will be our best move to capture him by yelling for a few men to come up to where we are."

"Hullo, you!" was the greeting of Toby Ross, as that school-boy stopped and looked at the returned campers. "Have a good time?"

"Fine!" answered four voices at once.

"But," Toby continued, "I never thought there was that much stuff in Hen Dutcher."

"What stuff? What kind of stuff!" demanded Tom.

"Why, Hen is back in Gridley," Toby answered, "and, from the tales he has been telling, he was the whole life and safety of your crowd out in the forest."

"Come to think of it," Tom replied soberly, "I believe he was."

"Then Hen's yarns are true?" asked Toby.

"They must be," Dick responded. "Who ever knew Hen to tell an untruth?"

"Say, stop your fooling, won't you?" begged Toby. "What did Hen actually do out in the forest."

"Why, he ate at least his share," asserted Tom.

"And got his share of sleep," Darrin added.

"He also did his full share of housework," Hazelton supplied, with a grin.

"We're glad he had such a good time," Dick went on politely.

"But did he really do any of the hero stunts that he's telling about?" Toby persisted.

"Not knowing what he's telling about, I really can't say," Prescott answered.

"What is Hen claiming to have done, anyway?" Darrin inquired.

"Oh, Hen says—but come along and hear him for yourselves," Toby finished. "Hen is just a little way down the street, holding forth to a lot of fellows."

"Come along, then," nodded Tom. "Perhaps we can slip in behind Hen without his seeing us, and then we'll know all that he did while we were snowbound."

Toby piloted them. A block and a half down Main Street a group of some twenty Grammar School boys stood, gathered closely around a central object. When Dick and his chums slipped up to the outer edge of the crowd they discovered that central object to be Hen Dutcher, whose back was turned to them.

Though Hen didn't know who was now near him, several of the other boys did, and they passed the wink.

"Hen, tell us again just how it was that you cowed Mr. Fits when he first showed up at the cabin," urged one of the juvenile bystanders.

"Huh! There wasn't much to cow," retorted Hen airily. "Dick Prescott and his chums were pretty well scared, I can tell you. But there was an air rifle standing in the corner, and I knew I could get it if I needed it. So, when Fits ordered Dick Prescott to get him some supper, and Dick was just going to do it, I stepped up, as cool as anything, and I said: 'No, sir;

Dick Prescott won't get you any supper in this camp. You'll get out of here, mister,' says I, 'and you'll be quick about it, too.' Well, when Fits looked into my eyes and saw that he couldn't scare me any, he began to whine, and says: 'All right, sir; I won't insist about any supper, but I must sleep here to-night. I'd freeze to death out in the big snowstorm.' 'You won't sleep here, any more than you'll eat here,' says I to Fits. 'But you can sleep out in the cook shack behind this cabin, if you want to.' Fits, he tried to beg off, but when he found he couldn't, he just marched out of the cabin like a man and went to the cook shack."

"Was Fits the one who set fire to the cook shack?" asked another boy in the crowd.

"I—er—I'm not going to tell you anything about that," retorted Hen, trying to conceal his embarrassment under an air of mystery.

"But say, Hen," put in another boy, across the crowd, after winking at Dick, "I really don't see how you could help being scared when you heard those ghost noises the first time."

"Huh! Me? Scared?" responded Dutcher indignantly. "No, sir! Being scared isn't in my line. But the other fellows were tremendously scared. I told 'em, again and again, that the noises were wholly human, and that we hadn't any call to be afraid of any man who used his voice, instead of his hands, against us."

"Was Dick Prescott much scared?" asked one of the auditors, with a quick side glance at Dick.

"Was he?" repeated Hen. "Huh! But, after all, Tom Reade was the biggest boo—"

Here Reade could control himself no longer. His deep chuckle broke on the night air, causing Hen Dutcher to turn with a start.

"Go on, Hen!" Tom encouraged him. "Go on and tell all about it. I'll admit that I was scared. So were all the rest of our crowd. I guess, Hen, you really were the only brave one in the cabin when the blood curdling noises broke loose on us and spoiled our night's sleep."

"Well, I wasn't scared, was I?" challenged Dutcher.

Hen's eye roved until it rested on Dick's face.

"I don't know whether you were, or not," Prescott replied soberly. "I had too much of my own alarm on hand to notice just how you were acting."

"Well, I wasn't scared," Hen asserted vehemently. "And I'd like to see any one dare to say that I was."

"How did you come to get invited with Dick's crowd, anyway?" asked Hoof Sadby.

"I wasn't—just exactly—invited," hesitated Hen Dutcher. "But I was going through the forest when the big snowstorm came up, and—"

"And you made Prescott's crowd invite you into the cabin?" pressed Spoff Henderson.

"Ye-es," claimed Hen reluctantly.

"What have you got to say about all this yarn, Dick Prescott?" called Wrecker Lane.

"Why, from all we've heard," Dick answered dryly, "I don't see any need of adding anything to Hen's story of events. He seems capable of telling all about it himself."

"And Hen really was brave when Mr. Fits was around?"

"He says so, doesn't he?" inquired Dick.

Several laughs answered this question, and Hen began to fidget.

"I wonder what has become of Fits, anyway?" suggested Ned Allen.

"We saw him here in Gridley, not ten minutes ago," broke in Dave Darrin. "We notified the police, too."

"Is that right?" demanded a dozen boys at once.

"Yes," nodded Dick.

"And Fits knocked Dick down," said Harry Hazelton, "but," continued he, "maybe it was that Dutcher boy that he was really looking for."

Hen's face became very pallid and his jaw dropped. He didn't look the hero that he had been claiming to be a minute before. Most of the boys in the crowd began to laugh.

"I've a good mind to tell the crowd that Hen really came out to the forest to help Fred Ripley's crew against us," whispered Harry in Prescott's ear.

"Don't you do it," Dick warned him sternly. "We don't have to blab. Give Hen Dutcher a little time and he'll let it all out himself, without meaning to do it."

"Sa-ay, weren't—weren't you stringing me about—Mr. Fits?" Hen questioned.

"Say, you fellows—hustle!" breathed Greg excitedly, as he joined the crowd. "There's Mr. Fits over at the corner opposite. There—he's turning and running down Abbott Street!"

Like a shot the crowd of boys wheeled and was off in chase. But Hen didn't go with them. Toby Ross, who brought up the rear, saw young Dutcher turn and speed homeward as fast as his legs would carry him.

H. Irving Hancock

CHAPTER XXIII

"THIS TIME IS AS GOOD AS ANY OTHER"

"There he is!" breathed Greg, who ran with the foremost rank of pursuing boys, as they turned into Abbott Street.

A policeman saw the commotion and ran fast after the crowd of youngsters. As the officer caught up with Ross he found out that they were "chasing Fits."

Though the man ahead ran rapidly, the foremost boys gradually overtook him. The policeman, too, was well in the front of the running.

Then the fugitive stumbled and fell to the ground. He sat up, but made no further move to get away.

"I may as well give meself up," remarked the recent fugitive resignedly. "The law is always sure to git a feller."

"Why, this isn't Mr. Fits!" ejaculated Dick and Greg in the same accent of disgust.

"Who's going to gimme fits?" demanded the man, looking stupidly about him, while the crowd circled him and the policeman peered down into his face. "Who's going to gimme fits, I ask? Will it be Jack Ryan?"

"This fellow is Dock Breslin, a teamster," muttered the policeman disgustedly. "Who said it was the thief that the chief wants so badly?"

"I—I thought it was, when I saw him," stammered Greg Holmes, rather abashed now. "He's the same build as Fits, and looked like him at a distance. And this man, Breslin, was peering around the corner and acting suspiciously. He ran away, too, when we started after him."

"I'll go with ye, peaceable like," promised Dock Breslin, getting upon his feet and addressing the blue coated one. "'Twas Jack himself swore out the warrant, I suppose."

"What warrant?" demanded the policeman.

"Didn't he swear out one?" insisted Breslin.

"Who?"

"Jack Ryan. 'Twas meself that gave Ryan a big wallopin' this afternoon, all on account of a bit of a dispute we had. Jack swore he'd be even with me, and I heard he'd sworn out a warrant against me," explained Breslin, who had the air of one stupidly rejoicing that his suspense was ended.

"I heard of no warrant for you, Dock, when the night watch had the orders read before we came out to-night," replied the policeman.

"Then Jack didn't do it?" demanded Breslin.

"If he did, he didn't let the police know about it," laughed the policeman. "If there'd been a warrant against you, Dock, the orders would have been read to the night watch at the station house. Did you run from the boys because you thought there was a warrant against you?"

"I did," the teamster admitted.

"Then Jack Ryan will be laughing at you to-morrow," grinned the officer. "Go home, Breslin, and behave yourself. Boys, you'd better scatter."

It was not long after that that Gridley Grammar School boys were at home and in bed. By morning they were on the street again, as there was still some of the holiday vacation left.

There was news, too, this morning. The Dodge house had been entered late in the night, but the Dodge coachman, returning late, had caught sight of a burglar near an open dining room window. In investigating more closely the coachman had scared the burglar, who leaped from the window, struck the coachman over the head, and then vanished. But the coachman's description of his assailant tallied with the personal appearance of Mr. Fits.

"Then the bold scoundrel is still operating in Gridley?" passed from mouth to mouth. "What nerve!"

"The thief is likely to stay here for a night or two longer," the chief of police warned business men along Main Street. "The truth appears to be that the rascal whom the boys have named Mr. Fits is without funds to get away. The loot that Dick & Co. found out at the camp was what the scoundrel had expected to take away with him and sell. That stuff not being in his possession, he must steal something else on which to raise money before he can go far from here."

"Why doesn't the rascal try some other town, then, where

he's not as well known?" inquired Mr. Dodge.

"Because he has houses that he and his confederates, now locked up in jail, had spotted for robbery," replied the police chief. "Burglars don't usually enter a house until they've looked it well over and know just about what they expect to find. I'll have all my men alert to-night, and well to do people will do well to be on the lookout, too. As soon as this 'Mr. Fits' gets loot enough he'll probably leave Gridley."

That same forenoon Dick, Dave and Tom, acting as a self-appointed committee, called on Lawyer Ripley at that gentleman's office. They thanked the lawyer for the use of the camp, and mentioned the burning down of the cook shack.

Hardly had they begun to speak when Fred Ripley sauntered into his father's office. Silently Fred stepped over to a part of the office that lay behind his father's back.

"How did the fire happen?" inquired the lawyer. "Some of you young men just a bit frisky and careless?"

Fred, from behind his father, scowled at the three Grammar School boys. It was plain enough that he dreaded having his father told the truth. Nor did Dick and his chums want to tell if it could be avoided. They had all of a schoolboy's aversion to carrying tales.

"No, sir; it wasn't carelessness on the part of any of our party," Prescott answered truthfully.

"Oh, well, it doesn't matter, at any rate," the lawyer assured them. "The whole camp is worth nothing in these days, and the shack was the least valuable part of all. If it's burned down, then it's gone. Mrs. Dexter wouldn't want any of you boys made uncomfortable over the affair for a moment, so you needn't tell me another word about it. But the cabin is still standing, and you may want to use it again. As Mrs. Dexter's attorney and agent, I offer you the use of it at any time when you please. You needn't even come to ask my permission. The use of the cabin belongs solely to you boys, and it's yours at any time without asking."

Dick & Co. took their leave promptly, and Fred escaped, for the time being, an investigation by his stern father.

"I hear that word is going around to the wealthy people in town to look out for Mr. Fits to-night," remarked Tom, as the trio of Grammar School boys returned to the street.

"That lets our families out," laughed Dick.

"Are you so very sure of that?" Dave inquired. "Fits might pay one of our homes a visit by way of revenge—yours, for instance, Dick."

"I don't believe he'll do it, just for revenge," Prescott replied, with a shake of his head. "Fits is probably superstitious, and he has most likely come to the conclusion that he runs to bad luck in pursuing our crowd. All of his ill luck, and that of his confederates, now in jail, has come through bothering us."

"Don't be too sure that you won't have another visit from the rascal," warned Tom. "Dick, Mr. Fits knows you're the leader of our crowd, and that's why he'll single out your house, if any, for a visit of revenge."

"I'd like to stay awake and see," smiled Dick. "Yet I'm almost certain that I'd fall into a sound doze before midnight."

During the day there were a lot of the Central Grammar School boys to be met, and each one had to have some account of the wonderful snowbound days. By evening Dick had very nearly forgotten the possible danger from Mr. Fits.

After supper Dave sauntered into the Prescott store.

"Dan wasn't out to-day," Dave announced. "At least, if he was, he failed to see any of us. Let's walk down to his house and see if anything is wrong with him."

Dick agreeing, the two chums turned down a dark side street on their way to Dalzell's.

At the darkest point on the street the two boys had to pass a collection of shanty like buildings, which contained a contractor's offices, a junk-shop, a second hand dealer's storehouse and a big stable in which the contractor's work-horses were kept.

"These old rookeries will go by when Gridley real estate gets to be just a little more valuable," grunted Dave, as he picked his way gingerly in the darksome spot.

"It's really a disgrace to the town, this place," replied Dick. "Hullo! Who's moving there? O-o-oh—say!"

They were just at the head of the narrow alley-way leading down to the stable. Up this alley-way a man had been picking his prowling way in the dark. At the hail from Dick Prescott the man turned, as though to glide back into the shadow.

But now, suddenly, the fellow wheeled like a flash and bounded into the path of the two Grammar School boys.

H. Irving Hancock

"I reckon this time will be as good as any other!" announced Mr. Fits, with an ugly laugh that showed his fang like teeth.

CHAPTER XXIV

CONCLUSION

"Jupiter! But we've got you!" flared Dave Darrin.

"Have you?" retorted Mr. Fits sarcastically. "Hold me tight, then. But this is a lucky meeting for me. I can settle all the old scores with you two. Yell, if you think it will bring any help to you."

"We know better," replied Dick coolly, though he was tingling inside. "We've got to handle you ourselves."

"Get busy at handling me, then," leered Mr. Fits. "Prescott, I'm going to begin by handling you in a way that'll make Darrin run."

"Don't you believe it!" retorted Dave angrily. "I may be killed, but I promise you that I won't run except to chase you, you ugly brute!"

"We'll see!" chuckled the wretch.

With that he reached out for Dick, who was standing his ground. Just then a lithe figure shot in between the boys and their promised assailant.

"Stand back, you hound!" ordered the newcomer angrily. "This is a matter for men. You and I will attend to each other!"

"Old Dut!" breathed Dick Prescott in the intensity of his astonishment.

"Yes, it's I," announced the principal of the Central Grammar coolly. "This is more in my line."

Mr. Fits had been pushed back from the spot by the energetic fist of Mr. E. Dutton Jones. But now the brute came back, cautiously, crouching and leering.

"Who are you, anyway!" demanded Mr. Fits.

"Oh, I'm one of the town's schoolmasters," replied Old Dut dryly. "As for you, I imagine you're that doubtful celebrity, Mr. Fits—otherwise a thief."

"Get out of this!" warned the rascal darkly. "This is no place for schoolmasters."

"On the contrary," retorted Old Dut, as coolly as before, "this is just the proper place for me, for I've appointed myself to teach you a lesson, my man. Throw off your overcoat, I don't want to take you unfairly."

As Old Dut spoke he "shucked" his own coat, tossing it to the curb.

"Wait, Mr. Jones, and we'll get a policeman," urged Dick.

"Wait and see how badly I'm going to need one," returned the schoolmaster.

"This affair is none of your business," growled Mr. Fits.

"Yes, it is!" insisted the principal of Central Grammar. "You were going to attack two of my boys. If you'll go along peaceably to the police station with me, then I'll let you off from a thrashing. But don't try to run away, for I warn you that I've kept up fairly well the sprinting of my old college days."

"I won't go with you, and I won't run," uttered Mr. Fits defiantly.

"Then get off your coat, for I'm going to start in," Old Dut warned the wretch.

Something in the schoolmaster's eye and voice told Fits that he would do well to get himself in trim at once. Off came his hat and coat.

"Look out, you ferrule-tosser!" jeered Mr. Fits, and led off with one fist after the other.

It had often been remarked, in undertones by Grammar School boys, that Old Dut was fine at thrashing boys, but that it would be different if he had a man of his own size to tackle.

Right now Dick Prescott and Dave Darrin were treated to a sight that they never forgot. In point of size Old Dut was somewhat over-matched. At the same time his opponent was a younger man. Yet it looked like a battle of giants. For some moments Old Dut had all he could do to hold his own. He took severe punishment, but gave back the same kind. Then, all of a sudden, Fits showed signs of wanting to get away. But Mr. E. Dutton Jones followed him up persistently, and at last a hard blow stretched the thief on the ground.

"Don't try to get up," Old Dut warned the fellow, "until I announce that I am ready for you."

With that the principal put on his coat once more, while Dave, with a very respectful air, passed the principal's hat.

"Now, you may get up," nodded Old Dut. "Put on your hat and coat."

Mr. Fits obeyed, next remarking whiningly:

"As you got the best of it, now I suppose you are ready to let me go."

"I never let a thief go, if I can help it," Old Dut retorted, gripping one of the fellow's wrists. "We'll walk along together, my friend, until we reach the police station. And woe unto you if you start anything funny!"

So it happened that, within five minutes, Mr. Fits was turned over to the members of a rejoicing police force. At the station house Mr. Fits described himself more especially as being one John Clark. Whether that was really his own name no one in Gridley ever found out.

Clark took his arrest philosophically enough. Now that he was behind bars, with no help for his situation, he became almost goodnatured. Ere long he admitted all of the charges against him. It was he who had entered the Prescott flat and had taken away Dick's watch and the fan intended for Dick's mother. Clark told freely how he and his confederates had taken toll from the Christmas shoppers, confessing also that they had had a number of houses "located" for burglary.

The prisoner told, also how he had found a megaphone in the little "lumber loft" of the cook shack, and how, with this, he had improvised the ghostly sounds. He had also found in that loft the snowshoes on which he had escaped from Constable Dock.

Clark—Mr. Fits—went away to prison for a long term, and Gridley heard no more about him. The recovered stolen property was turned over to the owners after the trial. Dr. Bentley was so overjoyed at the recovery of his prized heirloom watch that he presented each member of Dick & Co., except the leader, with a silver watch and chain. As Dick now had the watch bought for him by his parents, he received from Dr. Bentley a handsome pair of racing skates.

Mrs. Prescott wore her fan proudly the next time that she attended a performance at the local opera house. Other Gridley folks whose property had been recovered by the Grammar School boys were equally delighted.

The reader may be disappointed that Fred Ripley was not immediately punished for his meanness to the young campers, but it may be remarked in passing that fellows of Ripley's kind are always caught up with and punished sooner or later.

* * * * *

Boys filed in from one coatroom, girls from another, at the stroke of nine on the following Monday morning.

Tap! sounded a bell, and instantly the young people in their seats came to order, hands folded on desks before them.

"Young ladies and gentlemen," began Old Dut, in his usual schoolmaster tone, "I trust that you have all enjoyed your mid-winter vacation immensely. I hope that you have brought back here refreshed bodies and minds. Have you?"

H. Irving Hancock

"Yes, sir," came from all quarters of the schoolroom.

"The report cards given the pupils on the first of February will show whether you have answered accurately or impulsively," continued the principal. "I shall not expect too great performance from you this morning, but I warn you all that I shall not be jovially inclined to overlooking inattention or skylarking. Master Dalzell, were you whispering?"

"No, sir," Dan answered truthfully.

"That is well. Any young man who has just spent many days communing with grand old Nature should feel it beneath his dignity to whisper to mere mortals. Master Hazelton, you are moving uneasily in your seat. Be calm; you will not have to cook your own dinner to-day. Miss Bentley, it is hardly fair to smile so knowingly. For aught of evidence that may be presented, Master Hazelton may be a very excellent cook. Only his late camping comrades really know—and I'm certain they won't expose him. Attention! Turn to page 46 of your singing books."

After the singing exercises had been finished Old Dut announced:

"Master Reade and Miss Kimball will pass around with this composition paper. Each member of the class will have twenty minutes in which he will write a brief but interesting description of something that he saw, and which impressed him, during the vacation just closed."

Then, for some minutes, all was quiet save the scratching of pens through the room. Yet Old Dut, expert reader of pupils' eyes and glances, presently cast a bombshell by declaring in his dryest tone:

"Any pupil who writes anything believed to be funny will be required to explain before the class just what he considers the joke to be. He will then also be required to laugh three times at his own joke."

Here we will leave the Grammar School boys—and girls—for the present. However, we shall catch up with them again in the next volume in this series, which deals with spring sports, adventures and mysteries, and with a jolly good round of all the phases of public school life that interest young readers. This next volume is published under the title, "THE GRAMMAR SCHOOL BOYS IN THE WOODS; Or, Dick & Co. Trail Fun and Knowledge."

THE END

Choose from Thousands of 1stWorldLibrary Classics By

A. M. Barnard
Ada Leverson
Adolphus William Ward
Aesop
Agatha Christie
Alexander Aaronsohn
Alexander Kielland
Alexandre Dumas
Alfred Gatty
Alfred Ollivant
Alice Duer Miller
Alice Turner Curtis
Alice Dunbar
Allen Chapman
Alleyne Ireland
Ambrose Bierce
Amelia E. Barr
Amory H. Bradford
Andrew Lang
Andrew McFarland Davis
Andy Adams
Angela Brazil
Anna Alice Chapin
Anna Sewell
Annie Besant
Annie Hamilton Donnell
Annie Payson Call
Annie Roe Carr
Annonaymous
Anton Chekhov
Archibald Lee Fletcher
Arnold Bennett
Arthur C. Benson
Arthur Conan Doyle
Arthur M. Winfield
Arthur Ransome
Arthur Schnitzler
Arthur Train
Atticus
B.H. Baden-Powell
B. M. Bower
B. C. Chatterjee
Baroness Emmuska Orczy
Baroness Orczy
Basil King
Bayard Taylor
Ben Macomber
Bertha Muzzy Bower
Bjornstjerne Bjornson

Booth Tarkington
Boyd Cable
Bram Stoker
C. Collodi
C. E. Orr
C. M. Ingleby
Carolyn Wells
Catherine Parr Traill
Charles A. Eastman
Charles Amory Beach
Charles Dickens
Charles Dudley Warner
Charles Farrar Browne
Charles Ives
Charles Kingsley
Charles Klein
Charles Hanson Towne
Charles Lathrop Pack
Charles Romyn Dake
Charles Whibley
Charles Willing Beale
Charlotte M. Braeme
Charlotte M. Yonge
Charlotte Perkins Stetson
Clair W. Hayes
Clarence Day Jr.
Clarence E. Mulford
Clemence Housman
Confucius
Coningsby Dawson
Cornelis DeWitt Wilcox
Cyril Burleigh
D. H. Lawrence
Daniel Defoe
David Garnett
Dinah Craik
Don Carlos Janes
Donald Keyhoe
Dorothy Kilner
Dougan Clark
Douglas Fairbanks
E. Nesbit
E. P. Roe
E. Phillips Oppenheim
E. S. Brooks
Earl Barnes
Edgar Rice Burroughs
Edith Van Dyne
Edith Wharton

Edward Everett Hale
Edward J. O'Biren
Edward S. Ellis
Edwin L. Arnold
Eleanor Atkins
Eleanor Hallowell Abbott
Eliot Gregory
Elizabeth Gaskell
Elizabeth McCracken
Elizabeth Von Arnim
Ellem Key
Emerson Hough
Emilie F. Carlen
Emily Bronte
Emily Dickinson
Enid Bagnold
Enilor Macartney Lane
Erasmus W. Jones
Ernie Howard Pie
Ethel May Dell
Ethel Turner
Ethel Watts Mumford
Eugene Sue
Eugenie Foa
Eugene Wood
Eustace Hale Ball
Evelyn Everett-green
Everard Cotes
F. H. Cheley
F. J. Cross
F. Marion Crawford
Fannie E. Newberry
Federick Austin Ogg
Ferdinand Ossendowski
Fergus Hume
Florence A. Kilpatrick
Fremont B. Deering
Francis Bacon
Francis Darwin
Frances Hodgson Burnett
Frances Parkinson Keyes
Frank Gee Patchin
Frank Harris
Frank Jewett Mather
Frank L. Packard
Frank V. Webster
Frederic Stewart Isham
Frederick Trevor Hill
Frederick Winslow Taylor

Friedrich Kerst
Friedrich Nietzsche
Fyodor Dostoyevsky
G.A. Henty
G.K. Chesterton
Gabrielle E. Jackson
Garrett P. Serviss
Gaston Leroux
George A. Warren
George Ade
Geroge Bernard Shaw
George Cary Eggleston
George Durston
George Ebers
George Eliot
George Gissing
George MacDonald
George Meredith
George Orwell
George Sylvester Viereck
George Tucker
George W. Cable
George Wharton James
Gertrude Atherton
Gordon Casserly
Grace E. King
Grace Gallatin
Grace Greenwood
Grant Allen
Guillermo A. Sherwell
Gulielma Zollinger
Gustav Flaubert
H. A. Cody
H. B. Irving
H. C. Bailey
H. G. Wells
H. H. Munro
H. Irving Hancock
H. R. Naylor
H. Rider Haggard
H. W. C. Davis
Haldeman Julius
Hall Caine
Hamilton Wright Mabie
Hans Christian Andersen
Harold Avery
Harold McGrath
Harriet Beecher Stowe
Harry Castlemon
Harry Coghill
Harry Houidini

Hayden Carruth
Helent Hunt Jackson
Helen Nicolay
Hendrik Conscience
Hendy David Thoreau
Henri Barbusse
Henrik Ibsen
Henry Adams
Henry Ford
Henry Frost
Henry James
Henry Jones Ford
Henry Seton Merriman
Henry W Longfellow
Herbert A. Giles
Herbert Carter
Herbert N. Casson
Herman Hesse
Hildegard G. Frey
Homer
Honore De Balzac
Horace B. Day
Horace Walpole
Horatio Alger Jr.
Howard Pyle
Howard R. Garis
Hugh Lofting
Hugh Walpole
Humphry Ward
Ian Maclaren
Inez Haynes Gillmore
Irving Bacheller
Isabel Cecilia Williams
Isabel Hornibrook
Israel Abrahams
Ivan Turgenev
J. G.Austin
J. Henri Fabre
J. M. Barrie
J. M. Walsh
J. Macdonald Oxley
J. R. Miller
J. S. Fletcher
J. S. Knowles
J. Storer Clouston
J. W. Duffield
Jack London
Jacob Abbott
James Allen
James Andrews
James Baldwin

James Branch Cabell
James DeMille
James Joyce
James Lane Allen
James Lane Allen
James Oliver Curwood
James Oppenheim
James Otis
James R. Driscoll
Jane Abbott
Jane Austen
Jane L. Stewart
Janet Aldridge
Jens Peter Jacobsen
Jerome K. Jerome
Jessie Graham Flower
John Buchan
John Burroughs
John Cournos
John F. Kennedy
John Gay
John Glasworthy
John Habberton
John Joy Bell
John Kendrick Bangs
John Milton
John Philip Sousa
John Taintor Foote
Jonas Lauritz Idemil Lie
Jonathan Swift
Joseph A. Altsheler
Joseph Carey
Joseph Conrad
Joseph E. Badger Jr
Joseph Hergesheimer
Joseph Jacobs
Jules Vernes
Julian Hawthrone
Julie A Lippmann
Justin Huntly McCarthy
Kakuzo Okakura
Karle Wilson Baker
Kate Chopin
Kenneth Grahame
Kenneth McGaffey
Kate Langley Bosher
Kate Langley Bosher
Katherine Cecil Thurston
Katherine Stokes
L. A. Abbot
L. T. Meade

L. Frank Baum
Latta Griswold
Laura Dent Crane
Laura Lee Hope
Laurence Housman
Lawrence Beasley
Leo Tolstoy
Leonid Andreyev
Lewis Carroll
Lewis Sperry Chafer
Lilian Bell
Lloyd Osbourne
Louis Hughes
Louis Joseph Vance
Louis Tracy
Louisa May Alcott
Lucy Fitch Perkins
Lucy Maud Montgomery
Luther Benson
Lydia Miller Middleton
Lyndon Orr
M. Corvus
M. H. Adams
Margaret E. Sangster
Margret Howth
Margaret Vandercook
Margaret W. Hungerford
Margret Penrose
Maria Edgeworth
Maria Thompson Daviess
Mariano Azuela
Marion Polk Angellotti
Mark Overton
Mark Twain
Mary Austin
Mary Catherine Crowley
Mary Cole
Mary Hastings Bradley
Mary Roberts Rinehart
Mary Rowlandson
M. Wollstonecraft Shelley
Maud Lindsay
Max Beerbohm
Myra Kelly
Nathaniel Hawthrone
Nicolo Machiavelli
O. F. Walton
Oscar Wilde
Owen Johnson
P.G. Wodehouse
Paul and Mabel Thorne

Paul G. Tomlinson
Paul Severing
Percy Brebner
Percy Keese Fitzhugh
Peter B. Kyne
Plato
Quincy Allen
R. Derby Holmes
R. L. Stevenson
R. S. Ball
Rabindranath Tagore
Rahul Alvares
Ralph Bonehill
Ralph Henry Barbour
Ralph Victor
Ralph Waldo Emmerson
Rene Descartes
Ray Cummings
Rex Beach
Rex E. Beach
Richard Harding Davis
Richard Jefferies
Richard Le Gallienne
Robert Barr
Robert Frost
Robert Gordon Anderson
Robert L. Drake
Robert Lansing
Robert Lynd
Robert Michael Ballantyne
Robert W. Chambers
Rosa Nouchette Carey
Rudyard Kipling
Saint Augustine
Samuel B. Allison
Samuel Hopkins Adams
Sarah Bernhardt
Sarah C. Hallowell
Selma Lagerlof
Sherwood Anderson
Sigmund Freud
Standish O'Grady
Stanley Weyman
Stella Benson
Stella M. Francis
Stephen Crane
Stewart Edward White
Stijn Streuvels
Swami Abhedananda
Swami Parmananda
T. S. Ackland

T. S. Arthur
The Princess Der Ling
Thomas A. Janvier
Thomas A Kempis
Thomas Anderton
Thomas Bailey Aldrich
Thomas Bulfinch
Thomas De Quincey
Thomas Dixon
Thomas H. Huxley
Thomas Hardy
Thomas More
Thornton W. Burgess
U. S. Grant
Upton Sinclair
Valentine Williams
Various Authors
Vaughan Kester
Victor Appleton
Victor G. Durham
Victoria Cross
Virginia Woolf
Wadsworth Camp
Walter Camp
Walter Scott
Washington Irving
Wilbur Lawton
Wilkie Collins
Willa Cather
Willard F. Baker
William Dean Howells
William le Queux
W. Makepeace Thackeray
William W. Walter
William Shakespeare
Winston Churchill
Yei Theodora Ozaki
Yogi Ramacharaka
Young E. Allison
Zane Grey